Bohemian Negligence

Bohemian Negligence

A MEMOIR

BERTIE BLACKMAN

First published in 2022

Some names have been changed to protect the privacy of individuals and their families.

Allen & Unwin
Cammeraygal Country
83 Alexander Street
Crows Nest NSW 2065
Australia
Phone: (61 2) 8425 0100
Email: info@allenandunwin.com
Web: www.allenandunwin.com

Allen & Unwin acknowledges the Traditional Owners of the Country on which we live and work. We pay our respects to all Aboriginal and Torres Strait Islander Elders, past and present.

A catalogue record for this book is available from the National Library of Australia

ISBN 978 1 76106 712 9

Internal design by Samantha Collins, Bookhouse
Set in 12.8/20 pt Garamond MT by Bookhouse, Sydney
Printed and bound in Australia by Griffin Press

10 9 8 7 6 5 4 3 2 1

The paper in this book is FSC® certified. FSC® promotes environmentally responsible, socially beneficial and economically viable management of the world's forests.

For my mother, Genevieve—the light, the warmth, and the balance amongst the dark, the grey and the unknown.

•

The most beautiful things in the world cannot be seen or touched, they are felt with the heart.

Antoine de Saint-Exupéry,
The Little Prince

Contents

Find a spot. Find a crack in the wall. Find the air whistling through an open window. Follow the sunlight as it moves across the floor. Find the silence between others' words. Sit in those cracks. Nuzzle in and wait there till it's over. Stare at those cracks till they become one, two, seven deep cracks and there is enough space to hide, enough space to make a new world.

I have spent my life finding solace here. In the times when there has been nowhere to go, these cracks have saved me. They have made themselves into mountains and skies and oceans and sunsets that I sail and climb and wander through. Imagination drawing worlds to hide in. Better than dreams. Better than life, even.

This is love

The room feels alive in the light and dark. There is a big four-poster bed in the middle of the wide and long studio and that's where I sleep sometimes. That's where I'm sleeping tonight.

The lines of the timber slats join the shadows in their geometric roads and find their way to the masking tape peeling off canvases stacked alongside each other, shoulder to shoulder, corner to corner. Reflecting and projecting, the moonlight screens films across the walls just for me. The leaves rustle and move and whisper secrets to each other. They talk in bright scratchy voices. Quietly hysterical. Headlights from passing cars stretch and drive towards this inner landscape—blinding the room for a second—and then receding with the sound of the labouring engine, trying to make it up the steep hill of Attunga Street. In the dark, the unfinished paintings start to paint themselves as the world outside creeps in and becomes part of what's here. Inside, outside . . . who can tell?

I watch the lines move across my skin and I lift up my hand to catch them. I want to be part of that. I want to be part of those night-time lines . . . but the lines on my hands are too soft and human to fit into this world of shadow and edge. I'm too small for something so large.

Dad is lying next to me and I can tell he too is not quite asleep. His breathing is not steady. He holds me with his hands and says he loves me. He talks of the stars and the universe outside. He pats my hip in a constant beat as I lie on my side. 'Off to sleep, my little dove.'

I can smell wine. I can smell dust. I can smell turpentine. I can smell distant sweat. I can smell the old sunshine from the day sleeping on the furniture . . .

raising its head in curiosity. I can smell his breath, I can smell his skin . . . I can't smell mine.

There are so many cracks to hide in here. I find one and pretend it is a hammock and I sway in it and look beyond the moon, pretending we are back in Fiji, where we went a few years ago before Mum and Dad broke up. They fought a lot but I didn't care because we were all together. The water was warm and we ate bananas and the air was so salty.

He pats my hip harder and I just stay still. I don't tell him it's too hard. I don't know what to say.

This is love.

The room starts to blur and my eyes want to pour with rain.

This is love.

My tears are hot and fizzy like a spa. Like the spas in Fiji. I'm frozen in those tropical memories and I'm frozen here. I hope if I just lie still, the hitting will stop but it doesn't.

This is love.

It gets harder. And harder. And harder. My tears hitting the pillow drown out the sound of everything else and the ringing in my ears turns to the song of birds. Pitter-patter . . . trill trill.

Everything goes black.

I'm swept up by the sweet skin of someone else's arms and through my watery eyes I can see the room getting smaller and smaller. Like looking back from the end of a tunnel, like looking through a periscope—swaying in between the moon stripes—I can hear Dad weeping softly.

Maybe this is where I get my sense of rhythm from. Maybe I'm writing my first song here. Maybe this is where my actual life begins. Maybe this is what I deserve. Maybe I am worthy only of this. If he is sad, I should be sad too.

Is this what love is?

hands.

Paddington Street

The colour red.

Red in love. Red in paint. Red in heart. Red in blood. Red in words. Red out loud.

I have my own romantic vision of how the moments played out.

Mum and Dad lay on the couch in his house on Paddington Street. Their bodies entwined . . . gazing . . . eyes reaching. Hands still. Their legs wrapped around.

The currawongs sing their morning song in the afternoon—a musical introduction. The notes coo across the creases of the lived-in furniture, and offer a word or two to the people in the paintings, paused there, looking into a suspended time, waiting to resume a lost conversation. The afternoon sun streams in through the windows, and the blinds cut the light into sharp contrast. They become stripy in the shadows like ferns in a forest, like the keys of a piano. Stardust is in the air, twirling in its own golden threads, giving the passing moments a density that is fragile and new and raw and exciting. Dad recites a favourite poem, his voice causing the dancing universe to bow towards them, holding its breath in time . . .

When bees are hot with honey-thirst
and hastening with the Spring,
When kisses are as strawberries
and Love is more than king—

When quiet birds have merriment
by waters brown and blue,
And little maids wool gathering
will murmur, 'I love you'—

When blossoms dance in carnival
to hearten maids and men

And kisses are as strawberries
who would be sober then?

Now the moon is rising early in the blue daylight, but the sun doesn't mind. And life begins here.

first memory

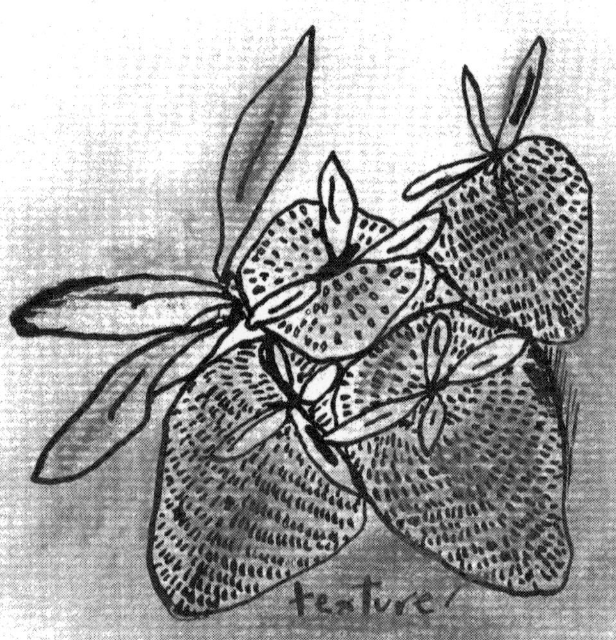

Memory colour

If you could touch your memories, how would they feel?

My first memory of life is blurry. A blurry red dot. A strawberry in a thicket of dark green vines and tall grass.

A chalky red pastel. A cadmium paint splash. A cardinal's feather. A lipstick smear . . . a strawberry kiss. All things red in one. I reach out to pluck the fruit but it's made of smoke and it vanishes as I touch it. It felt cool. Dewy. Tingly on the skin as if it were pressed there briefly and then it disappeared.

In the distance I can see our house sitting high on stilts. The long adolescent limbs are pale and glossy, with the rainforest's vines curled tight around them like long socks.

I can see the bottom of my mother's long white dress lapping gently in the breeze, but she is turned away from me.

I can hear cicadas chirping and birds swallowing their words and scratching for their breakfast. It's the first time I feel alone.

Fiji

My little brother is eating a banana by the pool. Its skin is golden like his hair and his mouth almost explodes with each bite he crams so much in.

Big blobs of sunscreen are dabbed across my mother's back as she tans in her pink one-piece. Her hair is pulled up in a loose bun. Dad saunters around in his blue speedos, using my orange floatie to play peekaboo.

Our French au pair, Berenice, laughs loudly and her black curls bounce as she speaks excitedly in heavily accented English. Everything seems to thrill her. Back in Sydney she had been looking after us, but we all got the flu and Dad wanted to cheer us up, so he bought tickets to Fiji and here we are.

It has rained most of the time but finally the sun is out.

I run around wearing seashell necklaces and nothing else, watching the palm fronds sway and hit the sunlight against the blue sky. The palm trees are not as green as back home—everything here feels more dry—and there are coconuts littering the ground beneath them.

On the bottom of the swimming pool are tiny mottled pebbles the same colour as the cat next door at home: brown and white and tan and black. The cat is much softer to pat, though. As I gaze up at the passing clouds I step off the pebbly step and my body drops into the hot bubbly water. When my feet touch the bottom I push up but the pool is too deep and I can't get back to the surface. The bubbles are loud and in my ears and in my hair and everything sounds muffled. I try to breathe but swallow water and I can't escape the bubbles . . . it feels like I'm falling down, down, down, down. I inhale and I can feel a burning in my chest. Everything goes black for a moment.

And then suddenly I can see strangers' faces staring down at me and I can hear their faraway murmuring. I take a breath and begin to cough.

They shrug and walk away.

•

The bathroom door in our hotel room is ajar and I peer in. Mum and Dad are fighting loudly. Mum's voice is shrill and Dad's voice booms back at her and they are throwing their arms in the air and pacing around.

I stay very still.

In the sliver of light coming from the doorway my skin is the same colour as the tiles on the floor. I am invisible here. I look back into the dark room behind me and listen as my brother stirs and sighs in his sleep.

Birthday barbecue

Pink and orange and blue balloons bump and squeak against each other in the breeze. It's already quite warm in Centennial Park even though it's early in the morning. A few cyclists go by but otherwise the park is very quiet. My brother and I are having a combined birthday party, and even though they aren't together anymore Mum and Dad are setting up tables and streamers together. While they are occupied, Felix and I run off and play chasings around the trees. I escape by climbing up onto a brick cube with a metal plate on top. While I wait for my brother to find me I look up at the gum trees and twirl my hands and pretend that I am like the leaves rustling in the wind. I often talk to the trees; I like to tell them my secrets. I think they are like ancient hands that grow out of the earth, and you can tell how old they are by the cracks on their skin.

The calm moment is interrupted by the sound of Mum and Dad raising their voices at each other. I look over at them and feel a tightness in my tummy. Then I am distracted by a *click-click-click*. I look down to see my brother gazing up at me with mischief in his big blue eyes as he presses a red button in the bricks over and over. I blow a raspberry at him and then, as I tilt my head back to look at the leaves again, I stumble and fall onto the metal plate, landing on my arm.

I hear a crackle and feel a searing pain. I scream and spring back, grasping my wrist.

I look down in horror and see that the skin has peeled back, crinkled, and it looks like a piece of cooked chicken. I can see smoke rising and realise that I'm standing on a barbecue, but everything seems to be happening in slow motion now and I can't move.

Suddenly I can feel Dad's hands lifting me up and away. He begins to run. The wind is loud in my ears and I can hear Dad's heart thumping in his chest as my head bounces against it in time with his steps.

'Come here!' Mum screeches. 'We need to put her arm under cold running water!' As Dad keeps running her voice rises. 'What are you doing? Where are you going?'

Dad doesn't answer; he just runs straight past her and puts me into the front seat of the car. I can taste my hot salty tears in my mouth. As he speeds off I clutch my arm, too afraid to let go.

We arrive at the local pharmacy and Dad speaks to the woman at the front counter. She hurries off to find cream and dressings, and then Dad holds me as she bandages me up. He is calm and I feel safe with him. I keep seeing flashes of my mother's face, shouting at him to come back, and I am worried I have made things worse between them.

We drive back to Centennial Park in silence.

As we pull up, we see that all the party guests have arrived, and they are being entertained by clowns in sparkly blue and pink pants who are bouncing around on bouncy balls.

The clowns make me laugh and I start to feel a bit better. Dad puts some beads around my neck and they must be magic because the pain goes away.

I look at the two cakes in the centre of the long table. One has five candles and the other has three. There are silver and gold balls and jelly snakes all over them. Everyone starts singing the birthday song but I feel shy and I long for quiet. I sit on Dad's lap and my hand finds his. I can smell his skin and his freshly washed shirt and the soft bark of the trees around us. I watch my brother who is so excited that he is running around in circles. He is wearing green pants that Mum made and painted with silver stars. He looks like Aladdin. I clutch the tulle of my skirt and tug on the beads of my necklace. I can see that Mum and Dad are not talking to each other but they are trying to be friendly to everyone else. Dad's eyes are watery when I look at him.

•

Over the next few weeks Mum changes the dressing on my arm and the pain makes me feel sick all the time. Mum makes me mashed banana with Vegemite.

She says it will make me better, that the vitamin B will help me heal, but I gag when I eat it.

Dad comes to visit more often and I wonder if I should burn my other arm too.

Number three

Dad is with someone new. She looks like Madonna. She's got a gap between her teeth and a round face like a dinner plate. She wears bright kaftans and white jeans and tight tops that show her cleavage. She just *loves* silver. Chunky necklaces in shiny silver, shoes that show her brightly painted toenails and big handbags with tassels that swing. Her laugh is a cackle.

Her long fingernails tap on tabletops and click against coins. *Tap-tap-tap. Click-click-click.*

She says she is a healer and asks if she may 'test' my levels. I shrug and say yes.

I'm sitting on Dad's tall wooden stool in the kitchen—Dad's sacred space, where he smokes cigarettes and gazes out of the window, reciting one-liners to passing birds and cats. His ashtray is nearby, but he is not.

She clicks her fingers in front of my face a few times, whispering to herself under her breath. I am curious . . . and a little nervous. After a few moments she announces that I am a bit anxious and I could do with a balance of the left and a balance of the right . . . And I need more vitamin D, too. She gives me some tiny white round pills to take. 'They're homeopathic,' she tells me. 'Take ten twice a day.'

I put the pills in my mouth. They are sweet and they roll around on my tongue like crackle candy.

She asks if she can call me Beats, and I say, 'Sure.' I ask if I can call her Mum, and she says, 'No.' Her name is Victoria.

She will be Dad's wife number three.

Musical stairs

I love walking up the stairs to Dad's studio. Each stair has a different note and my feet play them like a xylophone. Play it LOUD! Play it soffffffft. Play it meee-diiii–ummm. My legs are the mallets and my feet are the beaters and I am the heartbeat.

Sometimes I climb the stairs slowly and consider each key, make a rolling melody like the one my mum hums when she's cooking and listening to loud eighties music. Other times I run up the stairs with fury and haste to see how fast I can play the notes.

After climbing the musical stairs, my next favourite thing to do is to watch Dad work.

But I don't ever tell him I'm there.

I get to the top of the stairs and peer cautiously around the doorframe. I sniff the air. It smells like cedar.

He is painting.

Enormous white stretched canvases tower over his small, dainty frame. They go on and on down the room and onto the floor. He approaches them fearlessly, with a romantic twinkle in his eye and a bow of respect.

I watch the smoke curl around his hand as he slowly raises a cigarette to his lips, considering his next move. The smoke is the same hue as his hair and their hands curl together, silver and wavy. I love this. It's like he becomes what is around him. Smoky in his own making. Portal-jumping to catch the next splash of paint.

His eyes trace his strokes ahead of the mark . . . there is rarely a pause. It's like he can't quite keep up with himself. The brush can hardly keep up. It's as if his body is a mere puppet being moved by the threads of his mind. Graceful and gentle. Thoughtful. Soft yet fierce. Like a ballet dancer.

'You know, paintings paint themselves,' he would remark occasionally. 'I've got nothing to do with it.'

That always made perfect sense to me.

back again so soon?

Afternoon

Today I play a soft mallet song on my marimba stairs: the duck theme from *Peter and the Wolf.* I am wearing socks so the notes are short and muted and I am pleased with myself.

At the top I crouch down on all fours and peer around the doorframe. I can't see Dad anywhere but I know he's there because I can hear his voice.

I trace my way across the lines of the wooden floorboards and shuffle under a little table to get a better look. The sun is streaming in through the windows and hitting the little mirrors on the Indian stuffed elephants lined up along the shelf. Guardians of their kaleidoscopic reflections. A 'Bombay' disco.

Dad is with Victoria and they are lying on his bed.

He is on top of her. His feet are facing me and it looks like he is doing push-ups. I've never seen him do anything like this before. I have never seen anyone do anything like this before. It looks so strange. They look very tangled.

As the moments pass I start to feel uncomfortable and decide to announce my presence. 'Dadda? What are you doing?'

He turns his head and looks at me, a bit surprised.

'I'm exercising, darling. I . . . I'll just be a minute. Go back downstairs.'

He resumes his push-ups.

I feel embarrassed suddenly, and confused, because I'm not used to Dad telling me to go away, not used to being dismissed like that. I reverse on all fours like an awkward cat and make for the doorway.

Behind me their loud breathing joins the ABC news theme playing on the radio. It sounds pompous with its cymbal crashes and horns.

Perhaps I'll play this for my getaway tune down my song stairs, I decide. I take off my socks so I can be loud about it.

•

That afternoon it's nap time.

The stuffed elephants look at me as I walk past them. *Back so soon?* their mirror eyes ask accusingly.

Dad and Victoria are lying next to each other, sweaty and half-dressed.

I crawl into the bed.

Dad shuts his eyes and I scooch closer to him, until I'm only a couple of inches away from his face. I don't know if Victoria is awake, but I don't care, because it's just me and Dad now.

I can hear his breath whistling through his nose hairs. I examine his eyelashes, which quiver occasionally. They are black and go in all directions and clump together in parts.

I look at his mouth. His lips are dry.

I remember him on top of Victoria.

I wonder if it will ever be my turn to exercise with Dad.

I wonder if it will be my turn today.

I hope that it is.

I follow the lines of his wrinkles to the creases of his ears. I reach out, thinking to touch them, but pull my hand away and tuck it back under my side.

It's okay, Dad. Everything is going to be okay. I love you. We know each other—know each other like others don't. Maybe you were my friend in another world. Maybe we would hold hands there. Maybe I was your mother and you were my son and I could hold you and tell you it's all going to be okay.

I wish his eyes would open so I could talk to him, but they stay shut.

And eventually mine close too.

Spanish rap

I have an older sister and she lives in Spain. I don't get to see her very often, but she's the reason that I go to International Grammar School and learn Spanish. Dad stays up late a few nights a week to speak to her, and I always ask if I can stay up with him, but I usually fall asleep before the call comes.

I'm trying to stay awake tonight but sleep keeps pulling me into its tunnels with its long threads. As I climb down eyelashes attached to a giant sphinx's head I can hear Dad's voice boom close by . . . the clanging of pots and the kettle boiling. My eyelids flutter a little as the sounds imprint and double expose my dream, pulling me back through the soft dark into warm kitchen light, terracotta tiles, and my dad's bare chest and sarong.

The clock ticks.

The phone rings.

'Christa!'

My eyes spring open.

I can see Dad leaning sideways against the exposed bricks, twirling the cords of the phone high up on the wall beside him. He talks quickly and wildly, and I rise off the couch and walk over to tug on his arm.

'Oh, Beatrice Octavia is awake, Christa! You must talk to her. She can rap in Spanish now, you know. Beatrice!' He puts the phone in my hand. 'Show Christa how you can rap in Spanish.'

I put the phone up to my ear and it sounds like a shell inside. I can hear my sister's voice.

'Oh, hey, Beats!' she says.

'Hi, Christabel,' I say, a little nervous. 'I . . . I made up this rap song the other day in Spanish class. It goes like this. *Pantalones vaqueros tish boom boom tish / Pantalones vaqueros tish boom boom tish / Son azules son nuevos tish boom boom tish / Yo tengo pantalones vaqueros tish boom boom tish!*'

I can hear her laughing on the other end of the line. 'Very good, Beats! A song about blue jeans—I'm very impressed. Pop me back on to Dad?'

I hand back the phone to Dad and feel by heart beating a little faster in my chest. I was worried that I wouldn't remember the words but I did and the rush of adrenaline feels good.

I watch Dad's face as he talks jovially and I wonder if one day we will have the same type of conversations that he has with Christa. Maybe I'll be working in Egypt, excavating the sandstone heads of giant sphinxes and he will call me at 1 am and talk of sandy tails and laugh together like they do.

Suddenly Dad is looking at me and he's not on the phone anymore. He has that twinkle in his eye. 'The Dame Edna Experience is on TV tonight—let's watch. It's my mate Barry in a frock!'

We curl up on the couch together. Dad talks through the entire program, telling stories of the wonderful time they had in London, how they used to play jokes on people using lunch meat and cans of goulash, and how Barry looked better as a woman than as a man but not as good as Dad, because Dad had the skinny pins and slender ankles.

My ankles twirl around next to his, the glow of the TV giving us imaginary twinkly stockings.

I look at the clock and see it's almost 3 am and I've never been up so late and I don't care a bit.

Spaghetti lesson

'Now today, Beatrice Octavia, we have a lesson in life,' says Dad.

'First, you must rip two small pieces of paper like this.'

I watch as he carefully rips two long rectangles from a pad of paper he has on the table under the kitchen window.

'Now you roll both pieces into tight tubes, and then slide them over your two teeth . . . like this.' He turns his back to me for a second, and then spins around with his hands out front twisted in odd shapes with his mouth wide open.

'Dracula!' he announces theatrically, eyebrows raised.

Lowering his hands, he continues. 'Dracula is an expert spaghetti chef, and today he will teach you how to cook it perfectly. Muahaha!' He cackles in a Transylvanian accent. 'If you can cook a few things well, that's all you'll ever need in life. You'll impress with this trick! Now, take a seat up on my stool and pay close attention.'

I climb up onto Dad's stool as he strides over to the sink and lifts a giant steel pot from a hook that dangles above him. I reach for the pad of paper and roll myself two fangs. They are a bit big and loose in my mouth, but I don't care. I clasp my hands together in my lap, and watch.

'We must fill a big pot up with cold water to give the strands of spaghetti lots of room to be free—to be themselves. They like a chat, you see, and this will be their final conversation. But they don't scream like lobsters do; they just gossip in the fizzing, hissing bubbles.'

Dad reaches for the salt shaker. 'You throw some salt into the water for flavour.' Then he strokes his vampire fangs and turns on the radio. 'And we must have loud music to serenade us! Chopin, Beethoven, The Beatles.' He turns up the volume and a female operatic voice blasts through the tiny speakers, distorting slightly. Dad pauses for a long moment, considering the sound—I wonder what he is thinking as he grins, lost in thought, wiping his wet hands on his navy blue apron.

'Now, when the gossipy spaghetti gets very loud with its chatter, loud like the voice of the beautiful opera singer, you must check to see if it is cooked. You can use your intuition, but also you must do this . . .' He reaches into the pot with a fork and plucks out a long strand of pasta. 'You must throw it on the ceiling to see if it sticks! And if it sticks, it is perfectly cooked.' And Dad flings the spaghetti high in the air.

I wait, but it does not come back down. I look up and see it has stuck to the ceiling. There are a lot of other dried strands of spaghetti stuck there, I notice.

'Voila!' says Dad, beaming.

He transfers the spaghetti into two bowls, and then ladles two big scoops of steaming bolognaise sauce over it from a large blue pot that's been bubbling on the stove.

'Spag bol: you can't beat it. And that's the thing about life—you can't let it beat you. And the thing about life is . . . that life is about love. And love is all you need.'

He pours himself a big glass of wine from a cask that's sitting on top of the oven.

'You know, when I worked in Georges Mora's kitchen in Melbourne, we used to have a little trick. When the customers had drunk all the wine, and the cellars were empty, I would sneak around and drain all the dregs from the used glasses into empty bottles. Then we would slap white labels on and I would do little drawings on them. The customers would pay top dollar! That's friendship. That's art.' Dad slurps a big strand of spaghetti and sips his wine, holding his fangs carefully in place.

Drawing

Charcoal dust hovers in the air, thicker than the cigarette smoke he blows from his mouth.

A duet.

The sound of the line hitting the paper, scratchy and smooth at the same time.

'Now, Beatrice Octavia, did you know drawing is my favourite thing? There's no hiding in drawing, and I love that. We can use lines to make invisible worlds come alive. Like magicians of dreams.'

I watch as he puts lines on the paper. There is a glint in his eye. His breath pushes out his nose hairs and they whistle a little.

Hands appear. The back of a woman's head. Her neck. Her dress. The arch of a chair. All coming from somewhere I can't see. The sound of the drawing is like a second conversation we are having, and I listen carefully and study the rhythm of it, while careful to hold on to his words as well. Hoping to catch the secrets they might tell me.

Sometimes he pushes the charcoal so hard that it snaps. The line breaks for a moment, but he catches it quickly with a new stick of charcoal and I like knowing that nothing is perfect.

His lines are like his words. He speaks and the lines follow him. I am in awe of it. He smudges and creates shadow in a stark white world where there was no ghost of a smudge before.

'If you can't draw, you can't paint. So you must draw all the time. You can draw what you see, but what is interesting is drawing what others can't see. We can all look at the same thing and yet each draw something different. It's what's between the lines that's interesting—the space in everything. The mystery. The romance. It lies in the silence. The questioning. And what is beautiful is that no line can ever be the same. Ever.'

I consider this.

It's like a song, I think.

I think of the big painting that hangs in the living room. A woman arches her back with her hair streaming down like a river lost . . . A giant horse looks at her through an open door. His mane is wild like the woman's hair. Black and red and purple. It's dark and deep and if I stare at it for long enough it looks like the figures are moving and reaching for each other. Dad says it's about his nightmares.

Elohim
Extraterrestrials took me to their planet

Raelian

Victoria loves to go shopping. She always comes home with piles of bags. New dresses, jewellery, shoes—you name it. Today she's gone up to Bondi Junction and I'm able to spend some quiet time drawing in Dad's studio.

All of a sudden I can hear the soles of her wooden clogs clattering up the stairs. My muscles clench as I listen for the sound of the bags. But instead she is clutching a book, panting with excitement.

'I've met the most interesting man. His name is Rael. He is planet Earth's prophet, chosen by the Elohim.

He's from France. Did you know that extraterrestrials are real?' She looks at me, wide-eyed.

I like the idea that there are creatures living on other planets; my friends and I talk about this sometimes at school. UFOs are fun to draw, too.

'Well, I've thought about it, yeah,' I say. 'Sometimes when I see a shooting star in the sky I wonder where the aliens get such big bows and arrows from.'

She smiles. 'Well, according to this book'—her fingernails tap the cover of the book she's holding—'Rael was contacted by one of the Elohim, who took him to another planet to meet Buddha, Moses, Jesus and Mohammed. Everyone on that planet lives in peace and harmony, and there is no money, sickness or war.'

'What's Elohim?' I ask.

'Elohim are human scientists from another planet who have created life on Earth through DNA manipulation. Rael's mission is to inform the world of its human origins in anticipation of Their return. He has to build an embassy for them here and he needs our help. Needs *my* help. I'm going to help him raise the money.'

I notice that she is stroking her necklace as she speaks to me. It is a shiny silver chain with a big swirly star pendant on it. The star matches the one on the book she is holding. I read the title: *Extraterrestrials Took Me to Their Planet.*

'If you'd like to know more, Beats, we could have a ceremony for the Elohim sometime and you can see if you have a calling.'

'Does Dad have a calling to help Rael and the Elohim?' I ask.

'He's thinking about it,' she says, and purses her lips.

I go downstairs to the living room and find Dad, who's perched on his stool in the kitchen, smoking a cigarette.

'Dad?' I say.

'Yes, Beatrice Octavia?' he says absently. He is lost in thought, gazing at the pots and pans.

'Do you believe in the Elohim and that Rael man? The one Victoria met in Bondi Junction? Are you going to help them build their embassy?'

Dad looks at me sharply and his brow creases. 'I am absolutely *not* a believer in that crap. I'll never give them a cent. The lot of them can *get screwed*!' He takes a drag on his cigarette and exhales a large waft of smoke then goes back to staring at the pots and pans. His face has turned quite red.

•

The next morning, Victoria announces that she is going to hold a ceremony for the Elohim and asks if I would like to join her. Out of curiosity, I say yes.

I follow her up to the balcony, which is attached to Dad's studio, and find that my little brother Felix and Victoria's daughter Aimee are already waiting for us.

'Now, sit in a circle and hold hands,' Victoria instructs.

We do as she says. I look up at the daytime moon, which is half full, gleaming midway up the sky.

I think about the Elohim, on their planet not too far away, and wonder what they might look like. Victoria says that they love swimming pools, so I conjure an image of their village in my mind. White homes like igloos, raised up on stilts with pools attached, hovering in mid-air. I picture the extraterrestrials diving into the ice-cool water. They have shiny silver bodies and wear chunky silver chains with swirly star pendants, and instead of using words to speak they click their long fingernails at each other.

Victoria's voice pulls me back to the ceremony on the balcony.

'So we wait for your return, Elohim. We will build for you the most beautiful landing pad you have ever seen . . . a grand embassy, with vast swimming pools. Our most intelligent beings at the forefront—a superior community—and us . . . smiling and happy in abundant peace.'

She looks around at us and grins, clapping her hands together.

'Any questions?' she asks.

I look down at the wooden slats on the balcony. They feel warm under my hands from the morning sun. Sometimes I see Dad out here doing a wee and I can smell a slight waft of it.

'Can we have a swimming pool?' I ask excitedly.

Victoria huffs and looks to the sky hopefully, clicking her fingernails, as if they might arrive any minute.

'Secrets of the world Soup'

Oblong soup

I don't like going to school much. I mean, I like school, but when I stay at Dad's I'd rather not go because it means I can spend the day in the studio with him . . . or he might take me to the pub, and I get to drink pink lemonade or tonic water.

Today I get up early and go out into the living room in my pyjamas and wait for Dad to rise.

Soon enough, I hear his footsteps pattering down the stairs towards me, his bare feet playing a light rhythm.

I close my eyes and pretend to be asleep.

I feel his weight sinking onto the other end of the couch. I'm nervous and excited, hoping my plan will work.

'Well, what do we have here?' he says brightly. 'A little Beatrice Octavia. How lucky am I? I wonder if she is *really* asleep.' He gently tugs my little toe.

I crack one of my eyes open a bit, and see his baby blues twinkling back at me.

I pout. 'Dadda, I don't feel well.' I make my voice sound sad and croaky.

'In that case, we must take your temperature. Let me get my special thermometer.' Dad stands up and goes to the dining table. He opens one of the drawers and pulls out a box of round red stickers—the kind you put next to a painting when it has sold. He looks over at me and I quickly turn my face towards the window, pretending I haven't noticed.

'Now, I am going to take your temperature with this special sticker. If it turns green, then you are well, but if it turns red, it means you must be very sick and you will have to stay home with me.'

He takes a sticker out of the box and puts it on my forehead.

‘I’m going to count to ten and then we should have our answer.’

I take shallow breaths and try to make myself as red in the face as possible in the hope that the sticker will be red as well.

Dad counts aloud.

‘. . . nine . . . ten!’

He looks at me with a furrowed brow and takes his time examining the sticker.

‘Hmmm,’ he says, his voice grave. ‘Well, I’m afraid it’s not good news. That sticker is bright red. You must be very sick!’

I cough weakly. ‘But, Dadda, I can be bright-red-sticker sick and still spend the day with you, can’t I?’

‘Yes, of course, darling. Though I have a few things to do today, so if you’re *very* sick, then you’ll have to go to your mother’s.’

‘No, no!’ I yelp. ‘I mean’—cough, cough—‘I think if I just had the day off school I’d feel better. It’s not *that* bad.’

‘Well, if you’re sure . . . Today I have to go see Harold at the etching press studio and check on some proofs. But after that I can take you to the Imperial

Peking Afloat for a nice lunch. Some short soup will sort you out!'

I am beyond elated. I suspect Dad can tell I'm not really sick, but he continues to play along. And what is short soup? I wonder.

'You just relax here for a while and I'll make you some breakfast.'

I curl up on the sofa and gaze out the huge window overlooking Cooper Park. I can see into the neighbour's yard, where a woman is hanging out her washing. I notice the different tones of colour. Peach, pale blue, white and grey. The garments catch the breeze like the sails of little boats.

Dad comes back with a bowl of Coco Pops.

'This should perk you up! I'll go and get dressed and then we can get going. Maybe you can do a little etching at the studio, if there's time.'

The etching studio is full of shiny equipment. It reminds me of one of Dad's favourite Charlie Chaplin films, the one where Charlie gets stuck in the cogs of a giant machine. Copper and gold and silver glint all around. Piles of thick blank paper, big sinks, and a strange chemical smell.

‘G’day, mate!’ Dad says to Harold. ‘This is my daughter Beatrice Octavia. She’d like to do an etching while we have a look at the proofs. Then I’m taking her out for long soup.’

Harold is an older man with grey hair and he is wearing a blue apron with ink smeared across the front. He shakes my hand and his skin feels rough and callused, like the bark of an old tree branch.

‘Hello, Beatrice! What a pleasure it is to finally meet. I’ve heard a lot about you; your dad says you’re a fantastic artist. I’ll get you some copper plates to etch on—hold on a minute.’ He doesn’t say anything about the long soup, so perhaps he already knows what it is. Can you eat short soup and long soup at the same time, or do you have to choose between them?

Harold takes two shiny copper plates from a bench and puts them on the table in front of me.

‘This is an etching needle,’ he says, holding up what looks like a wooden-handled pen with a sharp metal tip. ‘Have you used one of these before?’

‘No I haven’t,’ I say nervously.

‘That’s okay, Harold,’ Dad says. ‘I’ll show Beatrice how it’s done. Can you give me another plate?’

Harold fetches Dad a larger copper plate and another etching needle, then leaves us to it.

'Now, we always put a border around our etching so we know where the image ends.'

Dad presses the etching needle into the copper and slowly drags the point from the upper left corner to the lower left corner to make a perfectly straight line. He then does the same on the other three sides of the plate.

'You don't need to press too hard,' he says. 'It's a bit like using a pen on paper really, but a little more slippery. You can draw whatever you want. Today I'm going to draw a pussy cat sitting at a window.'

I watch as he draws effortlessly on the copper. The curl of the tail. The flick of the whiskers. *Scratch, scratch.* The cat is facing away, looking through the window at the world outside. 'Easy as that!' he says, putting down the needle. 'I'll be back in a bit. Just be careful of your fingers—the needle is sharp.'

I look at my clean plates. Then I look at Dad's beautiful image and wish I could crawl inside his lines and feel what it's like to be one of his cats. He does draw a lot of them.

I decide that I will draw one of my favourite characters, Basil the wolf. In my mind, Basil is in his little home, getting ready to go to bed. So on the first plate I draw a picture of him at the sink, cleaning his teeth, under a low-hanging lightbulb. On the other plate I draw him climbing into his bed. Above his bed is a small window, like the one Dad drew. I imagine Basil gazing out the window from his bed, licking his clean fangs and thinking of a white cat he once knew.

'Finished, Dad!' I shout from my chair, rocking it back and forth a bit. I can hear my voice echo across the big studio.

Dad's curly grey head pops out from behind a big pile of paper. He smiles at me and comes over.

'Let's see what my little Rembrandt has done.' He runs his fingers over the lines. 'How wonderful. A wolf! Or maybe a cat in wolf's clothing?' He grins. 'The only thing I forgot to tell you is that all your images will print backwards, like a mirror image. But that's okay. In fact, it's perfect. The world we live in is backwards and upside down and downside left, so this is very insightful indeed. Maybe next week we can come back and Harold will press some proofs for you?'

'Oh, I would love that,' I say, clapping my hands together excitedly—secretly hoping for another day off school.

'Okay, mate!' Dad calls to Harold. 'That's it for today! I'm going to take my daughter off to lunch. We are going to float in the pink boat and eat some short soup, some long soup and some oblong soup!'

I lick my lips. *Oblong* soup? I can't wait to try oblong soup! I bet it's the tastiest soup of all.

catch a star with your dreams

Papageno

My dad lives in a bird suit.
It is also partly cat.
This could be his real suit.
Maybe his skin is just a disguise.
His feathers are drippy, smeary and splotchy, leaving traces wherever he goes.

They twitch and glitch in the breeze. Shine and quiver in the morning light. You always know where to find him—just follow his splashy trail.

I follow his inky crumbs like a hungry ant.

In the sun his whiskers come out. He purrs: content, still. And the feathers don't mind sharing him when his feline features shine.

His shadow can snap off at his heels. Slinking off towards the horizon. Gathering treasures for him. Lines and dreams for painting.

As he lies in the afternoon shade waiting . . . waiting . . .

The kitchen where he cooks. Clangs and bangs like a symphony. His tail is his helper.

Stirring pots in a question mark shape. Adding salt and splashing wine.
Sound and colour everywhere.
'The ink is the secret to the flavour. And tears make the roads to the heart. Put it all in with feeling.
In this soup, people will feel who you are,' he meows.

'Papageno, Papagena
Will you be my love forever?
Will you be my turtle dove?'
He kisses the hand of an invisible friend.

Pass the paint.
Squawk at the moon.
Catch a star with your dreams.
Don't be afraid.
Love is everything.

I yearn to catch up to him.
But for now,
I'm happy to watch from afar.
Sometimes magic needs the space between. To dance
life like a cat-bird.

I only hope
That one day it can be me.

Tarragon chicken

My mother's mother isn't like most grandmothers. She doesn't want to be called Granny or Nanna. 'You can call me either Grandmother or Jane,' she says. So I call her Jane.

Jane has a short, dark-brown bob, and she mostly wears black with the occasional splash of colour—usually red.

'There are many shades of black,' she says, 'and I am always hunting for the perfect, blackest black. It's very hard to find.'

She lives in a big old house on Jersey Road in Woollahra and everyone knows which house is hers:

number 99, with the white picket fence and the oldest, tallest palm tree on the street. She wears a bosun's whistle around her neck on a long strip of leather. It has a lovely sound when she blows it—soft and sweet. I can hear it in my mind when I think about her.

She loves everything French and everything Japanese. She calls herself a 'Japanofrancophile'. When I stay at her house she cooks tarragon chicken and prepares a salad of cos lettuce with a dressing made of fresh orange juice.

'To get sauce for the tarragon chicken just right, you need red wine *and* white wine as well as a bit of lemon juice,' she explains. 'That is the secret to my sauce.'

She sips from a tiny wineglass, and at dinner I get my own tiny wineglass and she serves me water with a dash of wine and I feel very grown up.

When I stay the night she lets me stay up late and watch SBS movies that are usually either French or Japanese and she is very happy about that. Sometimes I sleep in her dresser drawer because I am so small and it is cosy there and I feel like a mouse.

In the morning, she sets up her collection of Japanese gongs in the garden for me to play with chopsticks.

I listen to the sound of the trees and the wind and the cars going by and hear rhythms and try to emulate them. *Ting ting ting. Kling-tinketty-ting.* Percussion is her favourite and I can tell she is pleased when I take an interest in it.

She has a typewriter on her desk near the kitchen and she lets me type stories on it. The tapping of the keys sounds a bit like the gongs going *ting.* I look at the poems she has written and I long to be a poet like her. She loves to write about small moments that are curious to her, like lost odd socks falling in love with each other.

The stairs in her old house ramble up up up up to a cramped attic. The attic is packed with papers and boxes and everything from the past, and I love to play up there. Finding old bottles of perfume and mixing them together. Rummaging through buckets of old cassette tapes and leafing through photo albums. Wrapping myself in a sheet and pretending to be an Arab in a desert looking for my lost camel. When you lift things up it disturbs the layers of dust and the sun shines through making golden shapes in the air.

Sometimes Jane tells me stories of when she lived in Baghdad. Or when she went to Paris when she was twenty and lived in a tiny room and cooked on a gas stove and washed herself in the sink. She had been a secretary for a diplomat there.

'It was very unusual for a woman to go overseas by herself, unmarried. But I wasn't going to let what people thought stop me. I didn't need a man in order to live my life. I wanted to see the world and I did.'

She had had many jobs. Once she was a chauffeur in Sydney for a very rich man. She said that because of her small stature she needed a pillow on the front seat so she could see over the steering wheel. The rich man fell in love with her and proposed to her. She said it would have been very convenient to marry him, because he was rich, but she couldn't do it because she didn't love him, and love is very important.

She talks about how her mother died from a blood clot during surgery when she was very young and how she misses her still. Her father blamed Jane for her mother's death for some reason, and he was just very sad after that. She says she has always loved the water and wanted to be a sailor. That she loved to dress like a man but she didn't want to *be* a man. That her father had cut her off when she had children with my grandfather because they weren't married. She doesn't talk of my grandfather Jean much, and I have never met him, but I know he was an architect who never got a degree and always kept a case of Veuve Clicquot champagne in the boot of his car. 'A case just in case.'

I think about what it must have been like for Jane to do all the things she did without needing anybody else. And now she lives in her big house full of all the treasures she has collected in her life . . . baskets and paintings and wooden spoons and whisks and branches and things with black-and white stripes and typewriters. I think about how she is strong and independent, and how she must feel alone sometimes, even surrounded by it all. I wonder if that makes her feel stronger still.

Knockers

Today Dad is driving us to school and I'm excited. I wake up and follow the echo blasts of the ABC morning radio down the hall, past the bathroom, past Dad's downstairs painting studio, and out into the kitchen.

Dad is perched in his favourite spot by the window, drinking a cup of tea and wearing a long pink floral dress.

He looks at me. 'Beatrice Octavia! Fetch your brother and Aimee. We are going to draw straws as to who gets to pick my bra size. Hurry up!'

I run back down the hall to the bedroom we kids share and announce to my siblings that they are wanted in the kitchen. 'Dad needs our help getting dressed. A very important decision needs to be made about the size of his boobs!'

Schoolbags dragging and laces undone, our gallop is powerful times three, and there is a stampede to get there first. We bolt into the kitchen and see Dad standing next to the fruit bowl. He is holding three straws.

'Pick one each,' he orders.

We all grab for a straw.

To my delight, I have drawn the longest.

'Well, Beatrice Octavia, it's your lucky day. What'll it be? Orange, lemon or grapefruit?'

I consider the shapes in the bowl. 'Umm . . . grapefruit! That's my favourite fruit.'

Dad snatches up a couple of particularly large grapefruits and heads to his bedroom, shouting, 'Big tits! Big tits! What a pair of knockers!'

We wait, breathless with anticipation.

He returns looking fabulous. He is wearing pink lipstick to match his pink frock, and two very big grapefruits are popping out from a slightly undersized bra. He adjusts himself. 'Alright, ratbags, *allons-y*!'

We drive to school in Victoria's bright-yellow Ford hatchback, and my heart is racing the whole way. I imagine the awe on my friends' faces when they lay eyes on my dazzling father and see how lovely he looks. We screech to a halt in front of the school gates just as the bell rings. I burst out of the car and Dad takes my hand. I've never been so proud.

Cairns

I look out the oval window of the aeroplane. My stomach turns as the wing dips down and I marvel at the twinkling sunlight dancing across the ocean. My brother twitches in the seat next to me and complains because he wanted to sit next to the window to watch the landing gear go down. 'Too bad,' I say smugly.

Dad has been living in Cairns off and on all year; he's been painting for a new exhibition there and we are flying north by ourselves to see him for the summer holidays. My new little brother Axiom is going to be christened while we're there, and the whole family is coming—my sister Christabel is even travelling from Spain.

Dad is waiting at the airport, wearing pink shorts and a Hawaiian shirt. He opens his arms wide when he sees us. I hug him tight. 'Hello, Beats!' he says happily, and to my brother: 'Hello, Flip-flops!' He picks up our bags and leads us towards the taxi rank. 'Victoria is with the rest of the family back at the hotel. We're staying at the Ramada Resort. It has the best pink lemonades in town! You can swim up to the bar and order whatever you want.' Outside, palm trees line the footpath. They sway in the wind. I see cane toads squished flat on the road, patterned like kitchen tiles. The air is hot like an oven and the sunlight is brighter than in Sydney.

Dad makes small talk with the cabbie. 'How ya going, mate?'

I look at his hands as he speaks—I feel like they talk louder than his voice sometimes, making big strokes in the air like an orchestra conductor. I look at my hands; I have a bent pinky, just like Dad. My brother has the bent pinky too; it's a Blackman family trait.

The cab pulls up outside the hotel. As we enter, staff in turquoise uniforms greet me and Felix and welcome Dad back. They take our bags.

'Let's go out to the pool, kids,' says Dad. 'It's almost lunchtime. You can have a club sandwich. Steak sandwich. Hamburger. Oysters. The lot. Whatever you want, whenever you want!'

I skip out to the pool and see a woman with a wide-brimmed hat and big sunglasses lying beside the pool. She looks over and smiles, exposing the big gap between her front teeth. It's Victoria. Aimee springs up from beside her and runs over, squeezing us enthusiastically.

'Axiom is with the babysitter,' says Dad. 'Auguste, Barnaby and Christabel will be here tomorrow.'

A waiter comes over and Dad orders three pink lemonades and a beer. Victoria looks up from her magazine and says, 'And I'll have a gin and tonic.'

Felix, Aimee and I play in the pool all afternoon, dizzy from the pink fizzy drinks and the endless trays of hot chips. There are lots of other children around but we keep to ourselves. I love swimming up to the bar in the middle of the pool and sitting on the stool, pretending to be an adult ordering a drink. I ask for a pink umbrella and swizzle it in the ice, and then swim around the pool holding my glass high above my head, trying not to spill the precious liquid.

By the time the sun starts to sink in the sky, my limbs feel heavy and exhausted from all the action and sugar. Dad announces that it's time to go back to our rooms for a nap. We trail down the long corridors, shivering in the air conditioning, until we find our room. Dad walks in ahead of us and goes straight to the minibar. He proceeds to unscrew every little bottle one by one, draining the contents thirstily. He sways a little, then walks through another door to the adjoining room and passes out on the bed. I turn on the TV and watch the advertisements for crocodile parks and butterfly sanctuaries. I go to the mini bar and take a small yellow can of tonic water and a chocolate bar, things I would never usually be able to eat and drink at home with Mum.

A couple of hours later, Victoria comes into the room to tell us it's time for dinner. She's wearing a t-shirt but no underpants. Dad walks up beside her holding his penis and flops it towards her thigh. She slaps him away, hissing, 'Charles . . . no!' He raises his eyebrows, sways again, and staggers off. Axiom cries in the background and Victoria goes back into the other room to comfort him.

The evening quickly turns into night, and I'm aware of Dad and Victoria arguing on the other side of the wall. The room is littered with room service trays and plates of half-eaten spaghetti. I keep the TV on and look at the sleeping bodies of my brother and Aimee, their shapes stuttering in the blue light.

•

The next morning we return to the pool, eager for some more pink lemonades and maybe a club sandwich for breakfast. The air is already hot and muggy, and the hotel staff are sweeping toads out from beneath the deckchairs. Victoria is already installed by the pool, reading another magazine and sipping on a drink from a large pineapple. There's no sign of Dad.

Felix suddenly runs past me clutching his towel and squealing. He returns a few minutes later, drops his towel next to Victoria's deckchair and jumps back into the pool. I use the goggles I got for Christmas and dive down deep to follow his paddling feet, pretending I'm a dolphin. I clench my legs together and flap my feet and glide across the pebbles, running my fingers across the little bumps. I look for creatures that might be living there but there are none. Then I hear a shriek and bob my head above the surface. Victoria is standing there, holding Felix's towel, and there is brown stuff smeared all over her legs. She is hysterical. 'What is this? Oh my god, this is disgusting! Who pooed on my towel?'

I look at my brother and can see he is trying not to laugh. We both swim off as fast as we can. When we reach the other side of the pool Felix can't even speak he is giggling so hard.

'I . . . I . . . I went to do a poo but I missed the toilet and it went all over my t-t-towel!' he splutters.

'Let's get out of here,' I say.

We run back up to our hotel room, still giggling, and burst through the door, relieved to have escaped Victoria's wrath.

Dad is lying on the bed in the nude and there are tiny bottles all over the floor. I walk over to him.

He opens his eyes and looks at me and then shuts them again.

Felix and I find Aimee and waste some time knocking on the doors of strangers' hotel rooms pretending to be room service and then running away before they can see us. We race breathlessly up and down the corridors, hiding behind room service trolleys and hoping not to get caught.

By lunchtime my older siblings have arrived. Felix and Aimee and I are dressed in matching clothes given to us by Victoria especially for this occasion. The fabric is bright blue and purple with giant pink and green hibiscus flowers all over them, and it's scratchy and stiff against my skin. I feel self-conscious in the dress and wish I could wear a shirt and shorts like Felix. Why do boys get all the cool clothes? I wonder sadly.

We all sit around a long table in the hotel dining room. There are other families sitting nearby, but none are as loud or as large as our group. I look up at the enormous wooden fans turning slowly above us and wish I was at the bar in the middle of the swimming pool, sipping a pink lemonade.

I am sitting next to Dad, who seems a lot better than this morning. When the waiter comes over to take his order, he says, 'A dozen oysters, thanks, mate, and steak with Béarnaise sauce. Beatrice Octavia will have the same.'

The waiter looks at me for a moment, raises his eyebrows, then moves on to take the others' orders.

Moments later seafood platters and trays of oysters are brought to the table. I watch my older brothers Auguste and Barnaby talking loudly to each other, gulping their beers and slurping the oysters from their shells. Dad is getting stuck in to his oysters as well. I have never had an oyster before but I want to be just like him. 'Tuck in, Beats,' he says.

I put one to my lips and it slips into my mouth. I immediately gag but try to pretend to love it as I swallow it down, hoping my smile will hide the grimace. I look up at Dad, who has almost finished slipping his down, and I decide to just get through the plate by swallowing them whole. How can everyone love these slimy things so much? They have the texture of a golly.

I look over at my sister Christabel, who is speaking in Spanish to her daughter. She notices me staring and smiles at me.

My brothers yell, 'Time for the family song!' and the whole table joins in. 'Na na na na na na na na BLACKMAN!' we sing to the tune of the *Batman* theme. Everyone clinks glasses. We all sing it over and over again, ignoring the steely glances from surrounding tables.

•

That afternoon, as everyone lounges by the pool. Dad takes my hand. 'Let's go for a walk, Beatrice.'

I am excited to finally get some time alone with him.

We cross the road and I watch my feet, careful not to step on any squashed toads. The ocean breeze has picked up but it is still hot and my dad's face is red from the sun. We sit down on the sand and look at the water as the sun slowly starts to set. The sky turns pink and it feels like there's magic all around us.

Dad looks at me. 'Beatrice, there will be times when I won't be able to be near you. And that's okay.' He pauses for a moment as if to catch his breath. 'Look for me in the ocean. Each wave that laps the sand is a kiss from me. That will always be our special language. When you miss me, just remember you can always go to the sea to find me.' His grey-blue gaze is sharp against the bright colours around us. Then he stands up and holds out his hand. 'C'mon, little dove. Let's go back in and find the rest of the Blackmaniacs.'

Morning light

Some days at Dad's house are better than others. Lately, things haven't been so good.

One day I wake up earlier than usual and it's still dark. I gaze out my window at the stars and watch as they twinkle-talk to the rising blue. The blue that meets the black—a bit like the colour of the bruise on my knee. I hear the currawongs calling and know that night is slipping away and I should get up.

Rolling out of my bunk bed I land on the ground with a light thump. The house is eerily quiet but I know Dad will be awake somewhere.

I hurriedly pull on my school uniform so I can impress Dad by being ready so early.

I tiptoe out to the living room, and in the dim light I can just make out his shape sprawled on the floor. I creep closer, and see that he is naked. He is fast asleep, and smells like wine—a smell that has become familiar lately. I try to make a bit of noise by stamping my feet, but he doesn't wake.

The first ray of morning light hits the carpet near his feet like a ruler measuring him up. The room turns from blue to a pale gold in a slow glittery haze.

I watch as the strip of sunlight rises slowly up Dad's legs and over his middle to touch his face. His eyes open. He squints at me briefly then shuts them again.

Suddenly Victoria appears in her nightdress, Aimee trailing behind her.

'Oh, Charles! Look at this mess you've made!'

He doesn't flinch.

I look around and see that there are smelly brown smears on the walls, the table and down the stairs. I look back at Dad and realise it's all over him, too.

'Girls, could you help me clean this up? He's shat everywhere, and all over himself. I can't believe this has happened again.' She sighs and gets us all cloths from the cupboard.

I retch as I clean up Dad's shit, being careful not to get any on my school uniform.

As I wash my hands in the bathroom afterwards, I can hear crying and shouting coming from the kitchen.

I walk back out to see Dad now sitting on his stool in the kitchen wearing a pair of blue shorts. Victoria is yelling and waving her hands in the air.

Dad's face is red and he is looking at the floor. Tears fall down his cheeks. He looks so small.

I wish I could go to comfort him, but my body won't move. I feel heavy inside. I stare down at my uniform and smooth out the creases.

Family friend

There's an older man who lives next door to my aunt. Sometimes the man is leaving my grandmother's house just as we arrive for a visit. And sometimes he visits my mother to have a cup of tea. He's quite nice to me. I don't mind him. His name is Garth. He's what Mum calls 'a family friend'.

Garth is tall and skinny and wears tweed suits with matching hats. The man has long spindly fingers and his hair is white and his scalp is flaky. Maybe that's why he wears a hat. He has a moustache, too. He smells very strongly of old person's skin.

He drives an old cream car with brown seats and he has a fluffy white dog called Hamish who always stands up on the back seat and looks out the rear window. Garth's dog smells like him and it's possible Hamish is the same age. In the car there are tweed blankets—old friends of Garth's suits. They are woollen and very scratchy. When I ride in his car, I can see the dust on them and I don't like their smell and I don't like the way they feel.

This afternoon Mum is dropping me at Garth's house for a few hours. She says I can do my homework there and play with the dog and that she won't be long.

Garth's house is on the North Shore. The outside is white and it has a large front lawn. Inside it's quite dark and it smells like him. There are mustard-coloured curtains in every room, and in the lounge there are two armchairs with scratchy tweed blankets on them. The dog bed is in there too, also with a tweed blanket.

He has a collection of old blue English crockery that stands in display in a big glass cupboard—it all looks very precious. His garden is very shady and damp, and mosquitoey, and the bricks in the path are a bit green and slippery when I step on them.

After Mum drops me off, Garth asks what I've been up to at school and wants to know if I need any help with my homework. That day I had written a story about my home and it featured my two black cats. I had made a few spelling errors, but instead of scratching them out I turned the mistakes into little drawings of black cats and houses and trees. I'm proud of myself, as it has given my story extra pizzaz. The teacher put a *Well Done* sticker and two gold stars at the bottom of the page. I show this to Garth and he says, 'Clever girl.'

Garth says that it's four o'clock, and that in his house four o'clock means it's time for a nap. And after nap time we get ice cream with caramel sauce on it. 'How does that sound?' he asks.

I smile and say it sounds okay. (Mum doesn't let us have things like ice cream with caramel sauce.)

I follow Garth into his bedroom. He draws the curtains, then undresses and puts on a set of blue-striped pyjamas.

'In this house,' he explains, 'we don't tell anyone about nap time. Nap time is a secret time. I know you're good at keeping secrets, though, because you're a clever girl, aren't you?'

I nod.

Garth gets into bed and tells me to take off my clothes and get into bed beside him.

I undress and slip between the sheets. I turn my head to the left and notice that there is a crack where the mustard-coloured curtains meet. I can see the blue sky outside and the white clouds slowly passing by.

He gently takes my hand and guides it down to the top of his pyjama pants. There's a slit in them and he wraps my hand around what's inside. I don't know what it is and I don't want to look.

'If you do this to me, I can do it to you after—it will feel nice. Now, squeeze like this slowly until I say to stop.'

The air has thickened in the room. Garth's breathing has changed and it has a bit of a rattle. I just do as I'm told. I'm scared to look down and I'm scared to look at him, so I focus on the clouds passing and the light blue expanse. I imagine what it would be like to swim in the sky. I watch myself in the sky as if I'm underwater, diving into the blue and racing the birds as they swoop.

Garth grunts and then my hand is all wet. He gets a tissue and wipes it. 'Now it's your turn. You're a dirty girl, aren't you? You like this.'

I stay very still. I don't understand what he means. I have a bath every day and I don't stink like the smelly boys at school.

He touches me in between my legs and it stings a little but it's like my whole body is made of concrete and I can't move. I can't tell him to stop because my words have flown away. They are diving with the birds outside, too far away to reach.

He eventually stops and pulls his hand away. Then he gets up, takes off his pyjamas and puts his suit back on. He picks my clothes up off the ground and hands them to me. He sits on the end of the bed as I get dressed.

'Remember, this is just our little secret, okay, my clever girl? We don't talk to anyone about this special time we have together. And I know you liked it, so I know you won't tell. Now, if you go out into the sitting room, Hamish is waiting for you and he'd love a little pat. I'll get you your ice cream with caramel sauce. You deserve it.'

I walk down the hall to the lounge room. The carpet is soft and woolly under my feet and there is a big square of sunshine hitting the wall and floor. An afternoon sun projection. The dog is lying in the patch of sun. I sit near him and touch his fur. It feels like the hair of one of my friend's Barbie dolls. Under his white fur, his skin is very pink.

Garth comes back into the room carrying a small bowl of ice cream. He hands it to me and sits in his armchair. He watches as I eat the ice-cream. It is sweet and cold. I try not to clang the spoon against the side of the bowl. I try to be as quiet and invisible as possible.

There's a knock on the door.

Garth stands up. 'That must be your mother. Now remember what I said.' He pauses and looks at me for a beat and then goes to answer the door.

Mum walks in with her lovely clanging bangles. 'Ice cream!' she says. 'Well, aren't you a lucky girl.' Her tone is slightly disapproving.

Mum and Garth talk for what seems like a long time, while I stare at the geometric shadows on the wall, lying in the half-open eyes of the sun.

H
C

Ice cream

Mum has an appointment in the afternoon and tells me I'll be going to Garth's again after school. It's a few weeks since I was there last. I'm excited, because maybe this time my aunty might be next door with her cool boyfriend. His name is Bertie, the same as me. And he plays the bass. Everyone in the family calls him Big Bertie and me Little Bertie, and I like that. I am definitely smaller than him! My aunt and her boyfriend have a grey-and-white cat called Ponkie, and he's always rolling around on the gravel drive. He's very soft to pat, not like Hamish. I wish Garth had a cat instead.

We drive over the Harbour Bridge to Garth's house.

Mum doesn't come inside today. Garth tells her that one of the neighbours has some girls around my age and he will take me over to play with them, and Mum says she will meet us over there when she gets back.

I walk inside and put my schoolbag down, and Garth says that today we will have our nap earlier. The curtains are already drawn in his bedroom and it is much darker than last time. He has his blue-striped pyjamas laid out on the bed already—an eager second skin.

He gets changed and climbs into bed, then looks at me.

'Come on, you'll feel better after a nap. Take off your clothes and get into bed.'

I obey.

I look for the blue but the curtains are closed all the way. There is no cloud hammock to lie in or birds to swim with.

I shut my eyes and stay quiet. Garth takes my hand.

'You remember what to do. And don't worry, you'll have your turn after. I know that's what you really want. That's why I go first.'

There is a numbness in the air again and I think about my favourite movie, *The Land Before Time.* The theme song is loud in my head—like someone has cranked up the volume full blast. I can smell Garth's breath and his skin. My tummy churns. The wetness happens again and I lie still and hope that what comes next won't happen but then he's touching me again and it hurts. I dive into the world behind my eyelids and hold my breath there.

•

I can see light. I'm in a small square bath and the fluorescent bulb flickers overhead. Garth puts my hand in between his legs again and I look away. I listen to the sound of the water dripping from the tap—it drowns out the sound of everything else.

Then it's over.

He slips a bar of soap into my hand.

'Now, enjoy your bath and don't forget to wash yourself. We're going to the neighbour's house after this and you need to be clean for your mother. And remember, this is our little secret, okay? I'll get you some ice cream to have when you're out of the bath.'

•

I walk outside and the fresh air hits me. It is still afternoon. There are no clouds in the sky. Garth is wearing a brown tweed suit and Hamish is walking slowly by his side. We walk up the path to the neighbour's house and knock.

A blonde woman answers the door. She looks pleased to see Garth.

'And who's this?' she asks, looking at me.

'I'm Bertie,' I say quietly.

'Come and meet my daughters. They're out in the back garden playing on the swings.'

I walk through the house, which is quite chaotic compared to the neatness of Garth's. Toys and schoolbags are strewn on the floor. There's a big-screen TV with videos piled around it. A large kitchen with evidence of afternoon snacks spread all over the bench.

Outside is a neat garden that is just a swathe of green grass. There is an old swing set and two young girls with long blonde hair are playing on it. They are giggling. It sounds nice, and it clears my mind. The girls look at me and smile as I walk towards them. I look back and see Garth and the blonde woman drinking a cup of tea on the deck. Everything looks normal. I gulp back the feeling of the dark room and the sickly sweet ice cream still coating my tongue, and climb on a swing.

Snakes

I sit on the painted dark-green concrete step out the front of school waiting for Mum. I am excited to see her as I've been at Dad's all weekend. As the cars arrive to fetch the other children, I listen for the roar of Mum's old BMW. She's a fast driver, and I love it—you can always hear her coming. Eventually, instead of the engine roar, I hear the distant clanking of her bangles and see her hurrying up the street. I spring up to greet her and she gives me a hug. 'Sorry I'm late, darling. We're having dinner down at Hugo and Kat's tonight, so I parked over there.'

As Mum and I walk up the hill towards Hugo and Kat's house I tell her about my day. I've got paint on my hands from art class and I like the look of it. I show her, feeling proud. 'See? I'm an artist, just like you and Dad.'

At Hugo and Kat's I notice a new machine in their living room. 'It's a CD player,' says Mum. There is a pile of plastic cases stacked on the shelf beside it. I open one of the cases and gasp at the rainbow reflection of the round disc. I've never seen anything like it and I think it's magical.

Above the CD player is a huge painting of Medusa. Her hair is made of snakes and she has a determined and knowing look on her face. Confident. The snakes curl down from her head and cover her breasts and then weave into the mountains and sky around her. Snakes usually scare me, but here I like them—or, rather, I like that Medusa has power over them.

Mum comes up and stands beside me as I study the painting.

'Did you have a good time at your dad's?' she asks.

'It was pretty good. I saw Dad's face in Victoria's vagina.' I say blankly.

Mum goes pale and the moments that follow feel thick, and the lingering silence goes on and on.

'Darling, has . . . has anyone ever touched you?' she says slowly.

'Yes,' I answer flatly.

The room goes still and I feel numb. My ears ring loud.

Mum is silent for a minute. Her expression darkens even further.

'Who, darling? And where did they touch you?' She holds me by both shoulders, looking into my eyes.

'Garth does it.' I point to my pants. 'He touches me there. But he said that it's our secret. Our special time. He said not to tell anyone. I don't want to get into trouble.'

I can see by her reaction that something is very wrong. She releases me and marches over to the phone. Her face is upset and her mouth is moving but I can't hear what she is saying. I feel so small in the room. So alone. Like I'm dirty. Like I've done something bad. I don't like it when people get upset and it's my fault.

I look to Medusa and she looks back at me, raising an eyebrow. Ever so quietly, the snakes start to slither off her shoulders and head towards me. They twist out into the air . . . past the CD player and the towers of shiny new CDs. We watch each other cautiously. My body is stuck there. I can hear Mum's voice come into focus and the snakes start pouring as if they are liquid out onto the floor. There is a hissing noise that sounds like a bath filling up or a shower on full blast. Steam rises. The snakes speak. '*This is love.*'

They keep coming and coming, until the living room is filled with writhing snakes.

'*This is love.*'

It's just me and them in the room now. They rise to meet me face to face. They blink, and I blink back. My eyes start to water.

'*Thisssssss issssss love.*'

There is a new feeling rising in my tummy, one that I can't yet articulate. It's like heat and loudness and aloneness all at once—and I don't know where to put the feeling or how to fight it off. It settles on my skin like the steam rising in the room. I know it's here to stay.

The robbery

BANG.

I am bolt upright in bed.

Creak. Cr-r-ack. BANG!

The front door flies open.

Mum's footsteps hurry down the stairs. 'No!' she cries out.

Then her footsteps rush back up the stairs, heavier footsteps close behind her.

The carpet muffles the thumps.

I lie on the top bunk, staring at my bedroom wall.

Mum is on the other side. I can hear her whimpering.

Ringing in my ears. Thumping in my chest. This is really happening. There's someone in our house.

A man's voice shouts: 'Where's the car?'

Mum is crying.

'I'll fuckin' whack you over the head with the crowbar. Now, *where's the car*?'

'It's out the back. It's parked out the back. Please. Please.'

Thump.

Thud.

Thump.

Bang.

Skin-on-skin sound.

Mum sobbing.

Keys jangle. I am still.

Footsteps thunder down the stairs and disappear out the front door.

Silence.

'Mum?' I call quietly. 'Mum?'

'Darling, I need your help. Can you come in here? Don't be afraid. He's gone now.'

I hang my head over the edge of the bed and look for my brother in the bottom bunk. He is tangled up in his sheets, still asleep. I'm relieved that he's safe.

I climb down the ladder. Looking out the bedroom window, I see the sky is still grey in the predawn. The birds are singing their morning song.

I am shaking a bit as I creep out of my room and peer down the stairs. There are coins and buttons and jewellery strewn everywhere. I don't know where the man is. He could be anywhere. I'm afraid. My heart pounds in my throat.

I go into Mum's bedroom.

It has been turned upside down.

She's lying on her bed in her long white nightdress. She's pale. Wide-eyed. Her wrists and ankles have been bound with telephone cords.

'Darling, I need you to untie me,' she says.

I try to loosen the knots around her ankles but I can't. I am too weak. I try her wrists but I can't undo those either.

'Look at me, darling,' says Mum.

I look at her.

'It's okay. Everything's going to be alright. But I need you to do something else for me now. I need you to call out for help because the phones are broken. Go back into your room, open the window and use that big voice of yours. The neighbours will hear you, and they will come to help us.'

I go back to my bedroom and do as she says.

'Help! Help!' I cry out the window. 'Somebody please help us! Mum is tied up. Help!'

I hear tyres screeching in the back lane. A revving engine coming up the drive.

He's coming back.

I clamber back up the ladder to my bunk and lie there, frozen with terror.

Footsteps thump back in the front door and up the stairs.

My bedroom door is flung open, and a man walks in with my school uniform over his head.

He lifts up the dress, and our eyes meet.

His eyes are big. They dart around the room and then come back to me.

I don't look away. I can't look away. What feels like an eternity passes.

He puts my dress back over his face and steps out of the room, shutting the door behind him. I take a breath.

I hear him growling at my mother and her voice trembling as she replies.

He goes back down the stairs. I can hear him walking around the house, hear the crash of breaking glass, the thud of thrown furniture.

Eventually, the front door slams shut.

The engine revs, and I hear the car take off up the street, screeching around a corner.

When I am sure he is gone, I start to shout from my bed, hoping the sound will carry out the window.

'Help! Help! Somebody, please help us!'

I wait, but there's no response. No one can hear me. It's useless.

I climb down the ladder and return to Mum's room.

'Mum, no one's coming. What should I do?'

'Just have another go at undoing the cords. Quickly—I don't know if he's coming back.'

I am tugging at the cords around her wrists again, when: BANG! BANG! BANG!

There's someone at the front door.

I look at Mum.

She looks anxious, gnawing at her bottom lip, but her voice is calm when she says, 'That might be someone come to help us, darling. I need you to keep being brave. You're going to have to let them in.'

I take a deep breath and nod.

Standing at the top of the stairs, I am scared. Maybe he hasn't really gone. Maybe he's hiding, waiting to catch me. I feel the steps might swallow me up. I slowly dip one foot down and find the first step with my toes. The carpet feels scratchy. I exhale. Hold onto the banister to steady myself and peer over it to make sure I'm alone. Heart pounding in my ears.

The coast is clear.

I continue down the stairs.

The TV is gone from the living room and all our things are strewn about.

My school uniform is back on the bottom of the railing where I left it—I have a sudden memory of big darting eyes.

My breath catches in my throat.

Down the hall there is a shadow moving behind the glass of the front door.

I can't tell who it is. I don't know if it's him.

I move a bit closer and call out, 'Who . . . who is it?'

A woman's voice calls back. 'It's Shirley from up the road. What's happening? Are you alright? Can you let me in?'

My hand shakes as I reach up to turn the handle.

Shirley, our elderly neighbour from up the street, is standing on the doorstep looking very worried. 'Mum's upstairs,' I say. 'I can't untie her.'

I lead Shirley through the ransacked living room and up the stairs.

'Oh my god, Genevieve,' Shirley gasps when she sees Mum. 'Don't worry. I'll get your legs untied and then you and the children can come to my house where it's safe. We will call the police from there. Bertie, go and get your brother.'

I go back to my room and find Felix sitting up in bed, confused and frightened.

'You've slept through the whole thing,' I say. 'We've been robbed. C'mon, get up. Just stay in your pyjamas—we're going to Shirley's house.'

I lead him to Mum's room. Mum's ankles have been untied and Shirley is helping her off the bed.

I can see the deep imprints of the cords on Mum's skin and it makes me feel sick.

The four of us hurry back through the house and out into the street. The air hits my face, cool and clear and open, and I hold the feeling of being free close. The sky is still grey and there are brown leaves blowing along the ground.

At Shirley's house, I sit on the couch as the police interview Mum at the dining table. Her voice is faint and tremulous. She is still wearing her white nightdress.

'Yes, I think I've seen him before,' says Mum. 'I caught him trying to steal our TV last week and when I shouted he escaped over the fence.'

The police officer asks another question.

'A black crowbar. That's what he used to get in the front door. He said he would bash me over the head with it if I didn't do what he said.'

I flash back to the sound of his voice. The growl of it. I picture Mum in her white nightie, shaking beneath his raised arm, the back crowbar casting a long shadow over her face. I hear again the sound of the front door splintering open. My green tartan school uniform—how will I ever wear it again? The thoughts keep rushing through me.

After a while, the police officer turns to me.

'Can I ask you a few questions, too? I just want you to tell me what happened. Anything you can remember would be very helpful for us.'

'I saw his face,' I say quietly.

The police officer nods encouragingly.

'He had big darting eyes, and he was wearing my school uniform over his head. But he lifted it up and I saw him. His head was shaved. He was wearing a grey tracksuit with a yellow letter B on it.'

'Good girl, that's great,' says the police officer. 'Do you remember the colour of his skin?'

'Um, white,' I say.

The police officer is writing everything down in his little notebook.

'You are the only one who saw his face,' he tells me. 'Your mum said he kept himself covered with your uniform the whole time he was with her.' He pauses, pen poised. 'Did he have any other distinguishing features?'

I think about this, then shake my head. 'No, just his big eyes. I'm pretty sure they were brown. And he was skinny. Really skinny.'

Mum comes over and sits on the couch beside me. She takes me in her arms and I curl up on her lap.

The policemen leave to go and look at our house.

I look over at my brother, who is looking out the window to the back lane. I listen for the revving of the engine but there is nothing. The man is gone. But I can't shake the feeling that he could come back.

Lizard people

For a few weeks after the robbery I get to wear whatever I want to school. I don't like wearing my school uniform because it brings back memories of the robber. Wide darting eyes—that's all I can see when I look at the green tartan. I hear his gravelly voice shouting at my mother, hear her terrified whimpers.

I get to wear my pink tracksuit and it makes me feel better. I feel cool.

And I've been hanging out with my friend Lili more these past few weeks—she makes me feel cool, too. I like her because she doesn't care what anyone else thinks and that makes her seem strong.

Her mum is always complaining about Australians. How they have no style. How everywhere is closed when she wants to have a drink. How we are just trashy convicts. I wonder why she is even in Australia if she hates it so much. She has tattooed orange eyebrows and short, bright orange hair. Her skin is white like a vampire's and she wears orange lipstick. She looks like a Sherbie. Mum says she takes speed to do the housework, and I know she keeps money and drugs in the freezer—Lili takes the money sometimes to buy ice creams from the shops.

Lili's mum is out a lot at night. She's always going on dates with tattooed men with shaved heads who wear leather jackets and ride motorbikes. One night when I'm staying at Lili's house, her mum goes out, leaving us alone. We sit in Lili's bedroom and wait eagerly for her to leave. As soon as the front door closes behind her, Lili turns to me. 'I'm going to go get my cat Louis. He needs to have an operation because he's been very sick.' Lili disappears for several minutes, then returns holding a huge, and rather scared, black cat.

She hands him to me. 'You put him on the bed while I go and get the scissors and the needle for his anaesthetic.'

I lay the cat on the bed and pat him. He licks himself and purrs, oblivious.

Lili returns holding a blue razor, a packet of sewing needles and a box of matches. 'Oh, fuck, I forgot to go to the toilet,' she says, throwing her equipment down beside me and the cat. She goes over to a bright red bucket shaped like a small garbage bin in the corner of her room, opens the lid, squats over it and pisses. 'I always piss in this bucket when I can't be bothered to go to the toilet downstairs,' she explains. 'And I just chuck it on the roof when it gets too full.' She stands up and looks in the bucket. 'Like now.' She opens the window and empties the bucket onto the roof tiles. It reminds me of the sound of Dad and me doing a wee together on his balcony in the sun and I think it's funny that Lili does a similar thing.

Returning to the bed, she says, 'Now we need to shave a patch of Louis's fur so we can give him his needle.'

She picks up the scissors and cuts a few huge hunks of fur from the cat's belly. I notice there are a couple of other patches on his body with fur missing.

'Now we need to sterilise the needle so he doesn't get an infection.'

She lights a match and holds a needle over the flame.

'There. Now hold him down.'

She sticks the tip of the needle into Louis's belly. The cat yowls and struggles to free himself. A drop of blood appears on his skin.

'Stop!' I say. 'You're hurting him!'

When Lili pauses, the cat takes the opportunity to leap from the bed and scramble out of sight in a blur of fur and claws.

'Oh well,' Lili says, shrugging. 'He always escapes before I can give him the operation he needs.'

I look at her arms and see old scabs and scratches, no doubt the scars from Louis's previous escape attempts.

'Let's go outside for a while. Maman won't be back for ages and there are some clothing bins up the road that look really full. I want some new clothes.'

We pull the front door closed behind us and run up the narrow street, giggling. The night is cool and fresh and I have a giddy sense of freedom and mischief.

Up the top of the street there are three huge charity bins overflowing with garbage bags full of clothes.

'I dare you to get in the bin,' Lili says.

'No way!' I say. 'If I do that I won't be able to get out—I'm too small! Let's just get some clothes out of these bags.' I dive into the enormous pile, and Lili does the same. Ducking and diving like we are in a deep ocean, we laugh as we rip open the bags and throw clothes into the air. It's fun. We find a bag full of strips of orange and yellow Lycra and we tie them around our arms and legs. We look like gutter frill-necked lizards. And we hiss like them, too. Shrouded in our garment creations, we strut and shout from atop the mountain of bags. Pointing at each other we sing 'I'm Too Sexy', which is our favourite song.

A scraggly-looking couple emerge from the shadows and start shouting at us. 'Get away from our bins! This is our home, and it's our bedtime!'

We giggle hysterically, jumping up and down on the bags.

'Oh, *sorry,*' drawls Lili unapologetically. 'Sorry for wanting to make your home cool with our lizard disco! C'mon, Bertie. Let's get out of here.'

She takes my hand and we jump off the bags. We run down the street cackling with our arms outstretched, our lizard tassels billowing and propelling us home.

Mardi Gras

Mardi Gras is coming up and Mum says we are going to a party on Oxford Street at her friend Leigh's place. Leigh is a fashion designer and Mum has a few of her pieces; they are bright pink and yellow and made of linen.

Our babysitter Alex, who looks after us when we go to Dad's, takes us to the Rozelle markets so Felix and I can choose outfits for the party. I am excited because I am going to dress up like a man. We look through the racks of clothes and I decide on a brown tweed jacket while my brother finds a lavender hat with a tulle veil and a matching dress. The clothes are much too big for us, and we look like we have stolen them from the elderly couple who live down the street. When we take them home Mum chuckles at Felix's choice but looks at mine with distaste. 'You've got your father's dress sense,' she says dryly.

•

On Mardi Gras night Mum takes a photo of us out on the street with her Minolta camera, then we walk down Oxford Street towards Taylor Square.

There are people everywhere. Men dressed in leather, women with short hair, glitter explosions, horns honking, rainbow flags flying. Loud music is coming from all directions. The noise is unbelievable and the feeling in the air is electric.

I feel really good in my outfit, relieved that for once no one has forced me to wear a dress. Mardi Gras is not just about being gay; it's also about being able to express yourself. About being your most fabulous you.

Mum says I used to be extroverted when I was very little but I don't feel like that anymore; I just feel so self-conscious all the time. I try to pretend, but I feel a little bit like a chameleon. I still haven't told anyone that I like dressing like a boy. I'm not sure what it means or if it means anything at all.

I dig my hands deep in the tweed pockets. That's better.

I look at my brother, who giggles and looks around nervously.

We pass the Albury Hotel and there are drag queens dancing on the bar inside. I ask Mum if we can go in, but she says we are running late and we have to get across the road before the parade starts or we will be stuck on the wrong side of Oxford Street.

We wind up some back lanes behind Taylor Square until we get to a big old building that has metal stairs leading up to an open red door. We run up the stairs and the metal vibrates and clanks, making loud booming sounds that disappear into the thumping music coming from above.

At the top of the stairs is a huge open space like a warehouse. There are fashion photographs and drawings all over the walls and fabric hanging from rails across the ceiling. Leigh comes up to us and she has a big white turban wrapped around her head and a billowing white outfit. She has a big red mark splashed across her face and down her arms. I asked Mum about it once and she said Leigh was born with it, that it was her birthmark.

Leigh suggests that Felix and I go out onto the awning to watch the parade, and she and Mum go off to mingle.

Felix and I climb out the window to get a better view and I notice that we are the only children here, but it's not the first time we have been at a party full of adults, and we are good at looking after ourselves. I imagine what Dad would wear if he was here. Sometimes he dresses up like Quasimodo, the hunchback of Notre Dame. And sometimes when we watch Dame Edna on TV together he dresses up like her and flaps his skirt around, giggling and talking in a high-pitched voice.

Oxford Street looks amazing from above. It is packed with people and there is colour everywhere.

The parade begins with a roar of motorbikes ridden by women dressed in leather or white t-shirts and jeans and carrying flags that say *Dykes on Bikes*, and I think they look so cool.

Clover Moore drives past in an open-topped convertible.

Men with big beards all wearing black leather come next and I hear someone next to us refer to them as 'bears'.

After the bears come the drag queens. This year they have all dressed as frill-necked lizards in silver and rainbow glitter.

A few weeks earlier I saw the Baz Luhrmann film *Strictly Ballroom*, and my friend Morgan and I have been practising dancing in the living room. When I dance with her I like to take the lead. I picture myself as the lead character Scott, and in those moments I feel like I can do anything, be anyone. Watching the parade makes me feel the same way. I shut my eyes and fantasise riding up the front of one of the floats, wearing a tuxedo, and the bright lights eclipse everything that's around.

Buderim

Every holiday we drive to Queensland to visit our friends in Buderim, and this Christmas break is no exception.

Mum wakes us up at 4 am, and although I am tired I'm excited too.

We load up the orange kombi van, and drive off into the still, black morning.

The sky starts to open its eyes as we hit Mount White, just north of Sydney on the highway, and the clouds dapple the road. I open the window and stretch my hand into the cold, wet air, spreading my fingers out to try to catch them . . . but when I touch them they disappear against my skin. I've always wondered what clouds feel like, and now I know: damp. Not like fairy floss.

My brother's head is heavy against my left arm as he sleeps. I draw lines around the shape of Mum's shoulders as she drives, over and over, tracing the soft edges of her body, pulling the threads around her and out onto the road as it winds its way to a distant world.

The long neck of the giant dinosaur sign for The Australian Reptile Park arches over us, and I think of the brontosaurus from *The Land Before Time* and how cool it would be if they were wandering through our forests now . . . and what it would be like to live among them.

Mum hands us each a small packet of chips and I nibble mine as slowly as possible in order to torture my brother, who has shovelled the whole packet in quickly. I start to fall asleep on our shared pillow in the middle seat and hear him trying to steal my chips. As I snatch them back and tuck them under my arm, he screams to Mum, 'It's not fair!'

We stop at Macksville for lunch at the health food shop and all order the same thing: a falafel roll with shredded beetroot and hummus and carrot. Delicious. Mum would never dream of feeding us fast food, but we always dream of eating it. I guess you always want what you don't have.

We pass the Big Banana in Coffs Harbour but we don't stop. We pass the Big Prawn in Ballina, and I remember the time we broke down there and had to live on seafood sticks and potato scallops. Felix and I fight over who gets to rest their head on the front of the pillow and Mum shouts at us to be quiet.

Tracy Chapman is blaring from the car stereo. 'Fast Car' in our fast car. I love the tremble in Tracy's voice, though I'm always confused because on the cover of the cassette there is a picture of a man. I think of the police sirens flashing and the lines of the wooden floor of the apartment she sings about. The rain. The wet roads—it all feels as real as the road in front of us.

The light starts to fade and the black sky is chasing us up the highway like no time at all has passed since this morning.

'There's Buderim Mountain.' Mum points to a shadowy form in the distance. 'If we can see that, it means we're one hour away. Not far now.'

I can smell the lantana and hear the shrill of cicadas heralding our return.

'Where are we staying this time, Mum?' I ask. 'Will Robin and Charlotte and Shelley be there?'

'We're staying with the Robbs. You know, with Jennifer and Norman and Betty. The kids are all around, and they are excited to see you both.'

I love Betty. She's Jennifer's mother. She's very old and she's a painter. She wears see-through pants that go up around her boobs and a head wrap made of fabric she's painted. She lives on the same land that all her kids and her kids' kids live on, surrounded by rainforests and bamboo and with dams full of yabbies. There is a mango tree in her garden, and her grandson Robin cuts them from the tree for her with snippers attached to a long stick. He's clever. I like hanging out with him because he's also naughty and a bit older. He steals money from Betty when she goes out; she keeps rolls of cash in a white cloth bag. Robin says she's never paid tax. He buys cigarettes with the money and offers them to us. It makes me feel cool and grown-up when I smoke, but I don't inhale because it makes me cough. I like the taste and smell of them—it reminds me of Dad.

•

When we arrive, Mum sits on the deck with Betty and Jennifer and starts one of her long, long conversations. I hear the words 'Moon trine Jupiter' and 'Saturn is in retrograde' and decide to leave them to it.

Felix and I walk down the road to find Robin. It's dark. We are scared and we've forgotten to wear shoes. Suddenly a huge toad comes spinning through the air towards us and lands on my arm. I scream and Felix screams and then there are toads coming from everywhere. We scream and run. We can hear hoots and loud rustling sounds coming from the bushes and it sounds like a monster is coming for us.

Then Robin appears from behind a bush. He points at us and starts laughing. His sandy blond hair falls over his eyes and his skinny bare legs and feet stand out white and freckly against the green. 'You should have seen your faces!' He holds his stomach as the laughter roars out. 'You gotta watch out for those devil worshippers. The toads are the first sign they're coming. See those black shadows? That's them watching.'

Felix and I cling to each other and peer into the bushes, and I swear I can see a dark shadow flit off out of sight.

'C'mon,' says Robin. 'Come up to my room, and I'll show you what I've been growing.'

We walk up a steep drive that leads to a small workshop that has a makeshift shack on top. Downstairs there are freshly made clay cups and plates drying on racks. It smells damp and a bit like mud. We wind our way through the racks, then up up up the narrow wooden stairs we climb, to Robin's room. There's a single bed, a TV in the corner, and magazines and VHS cases scattered on the floor. It smells like cigarettes. Robin opens another door and shows us a room full of plants hanging upside down to dry. 'Check it out,' says Robin. 'Dad says I can grow marijuana and dry it in here. It'll be ready in a few months, and then I'm gonna sell it. You're too young to smoke it, but I'm gonna roll a joint.'

'Can we have a cigarette, then?' I ask.

Robin mutters something about bum-puffing as he hands me one.

I share it with my brother. I can tell he's nervous, but he smokes it anyway. The cigarette looks so strange in his slender feminine hands. Robin picks up a video and I see the word *Chucky* on the cover, along with a big letter R.

'Let's watch this—see if I can't get your minds off the devil worshippers.' He cackles.

I have nightmares all night.

•

When I wake up the next morning I notice two red bumps on my arm quite close together, and I'm scared that I've been bitten by a spider. I show Robin the bite and he shakes his head.

'If that's what I think it is, you're in big trouble.'

My heart skips a beat. 'What do you think it is?'

'It looks like you've been chomped by the fangs of Leonard,' Robin says seriously.

I stare at the bite, now quite distressed. 'Who is Leonard?' I quaver.

I imagine a gigantic insect coming down from the top of Buderim Mountain with fangs bared, hungry for the taste of city kids . . . and laying eyes on me, licking its lips and sinking its fangs in.

'Oh, Leonard is Dad's uncle. He's always drunk. And his favourite drink is children's blood. We all know he's a vampire, I've just been waiting to catch him in the act . . . and I think I've finally found proof!' Robin gestures to my bite. 'I can't wait to tell Ben—he'll freak.'

I run down the stairs and up the dirt track towards Betty's house clutching my arm, desperate to find Mum. I skid into the living room to find Mum sitting with Betty and Jennifer eating mango, talking loudly and laughing. They all stop to look at me.

I hold out my arm. 'Mum! Mum!' I shriek. 'Leonard the drunken vampire bit me and sucked my blood in the middle of the night. What am I going to do? Will I turn into a drunken vampire too?'

The women just chuckle.

'Oh, Leonard is a drunk alright,' says Jennifer. 'And he's too drunk to go around biting children in their sleep. He passed out in the garden last night and he's still there. Couldn't have possibly been him.'

I look to Mum for confirmation, and she sighs.

'You'll be fine, darling; they just look like mosquito bites. Anyway, we've decided to go to Double Island Point for a few days. Won't that be lovely? We can camp on the beach and you can go swimming. If everyone starts packing now, we can leave this afternoon. Go and find your brother and tell Robin to get his things together as well.'

•

There are four cars and we all travel in convoy to the island. There are more of us kids now and it feel like we are a tribe. The others know the point well and are talking about all the adventures they have had there, how the sand dunes are excellent to slide down on your boogie board and how the dingoes will circle our tents in the night.

We bush-bash through a rainforest and drive through a shallow creek. Jennifer remarks that it's lucky that we have arrived when it's low tide, otherwise we wouldn't have been able to cross. Through the vines and palm ferns, I catch glimpses of the crystal blue ocean. Our destination.

We pull up under the branches of some trees near the beach and everyone piles out of the cars. The sand feels good beneath my feet, and when I squirm my toes a little deeper it feels cool and hard and wet, and I wonder how far you'd have to dig to find the ocean under there. The adults pitch tents and attach tarps to the cars for shade, and Mum asks us kids to go collect some firewood. We run into the bush and start gathering leaves and sticks and stack them in pouches we have made with our t-shirts. I look at the older girls, who are wearing bikini tops, and then look down at my bare chest, and I am so glad I still get to run around like a boy. I don't ever want to have boobs. I like the feeling of being free. I feel strong this way.

Robin suddenly appears from the bushes. He's stripped off and has tied a giant leaf around his waist with a vine, and he has smeared mud on his face. He squats down beside us.

'Let's all dress up like forest spirits and go scare the adults.'

We spend the next few minutes finding the perfect leaves and washed-up beach treasures and attaching them to our bodies. Robin finds some long sticks and throws one to each of us. 'Your weapons. Spears for huntin'.' We paint each other with mud from a nearby creek and it feels good to have shucked off our city clothes and joined the twiggy branchy world around us.

In a whirlwind of excitement we descend upon the adults, who are already lazing about, sunbaking naked. Hooting and trilling we run around them in circles and they scream until they realise what is going on.

'ROBIN!' shrieks Jennifer. 'You scared the shit out of me. I was just starting to relax!'

Betty is reclining in her long see-through pants, cackling. She doesn't seem too fussed. 'How wonderful,' she remarks.

Mum looks at Felix and me, and I can tell she's impressed. 'Let's all dress up,' she suggests. 'You guys look fabulous!'

And so the adults too run into the bush and start collecting treasures for costumes. I can hear laughter echoing across the dunes as everyone makes the transition into their tribal best.

Down on the beach, the tide is going out and the crashing waves are receding. We all gather on the hard sand and revel in our foraged frocks. Betty is our leader, with the largest headdress, and she looks particularly splendid. I can see everyone exudes a new-found power, to be freed of self-consciousness, unhindered. We decide to do a photo shoot in our finery, posing for a family portrait. Other holidaymakers slow down as they drive past and I can see a few camera flashes go off. The same vans drive past again . . . and again. It seems we have become a tourist attraction. We enjoy hissing and rattling our spears at anyone who comes too close.

As the daylight fades, we all sit around the fire. We have shed our costumes and I am back in my board shorts. Robin is talking to Mum and Jennifer, bragging about how when he went on a school camp recently he had to steal a bunch of condoms because all the girls were chasing him, wanting sex. Mum and Jennifer shriek with laughter. It's the first time I realise that Robin must be more like a man than a boy, and I immediately feel a bit different around him. Shy all of a sudden. I remember what it looks like for a boy to be a man and then I feel sick in my stomach.

I don't want to be near it.

Memories flash.

Curtains.

Ice cream.

Blue sky.

Raspy breaths.

I tell Mum that I want to go to bed.

She's sleeping in the tents with the adults and Felix and I have dug a hole in the sand and filled it with doonas and pillows. I crawl into my nest, and my brother jumps in after me with a thud. Here I feel safe, contained. The universe opens up its arms, stretching out an enormous twinkling sky. As the stars sing us bedtime stories, I can sense Felix getting drowsy by my side. When the camp has gone quiet, I peer over the lip of the hole and watch as a little crab scutters past us. She stops with her pincers held high in the air, and begins to scoop little clawfuls of sand up and out. Burrowing down, down, down . . . into a tunnel below.

Bareback riding

Next holidays, when we are back up in Buderim, Mum sends me to horseriding camp with some of the older kids: Shelley, Robin and Ishani. I'm excited because I've never ridden a horse before, and I'll get to be on my own for five whole days.

The camp is about forty minutes from where we usually stay with the Robbs, and as we get closer the landscape turns from rainforest to rolling green hills and farmland. We drive over a cattle grid that makes the car shake violently and continue on past paddocks dotted with horses, looking relaxed and eating grass, shaking their manes in the wind.

We pull up to a big old wooden house and a boy of about nineteen walks out to greet us. He has patchy stubble and long sandy hair. He smiles. 'Welcome to Camp Shaktamundra,' he says. 'I'm Dave.'

Shelley and Ishani, who arrived earlier, appear from behind the house and shout for me to come and see where we will be staying.

I look at Mum, and she nods that I can go, so I turn and run off with the others.

'The boys have to sleep separate from the girls,' Shelley tells me.

Behind the house are a couple of small sheds lined with bunk beds. There is no other furniture and the wooden floors are dusty. I throw my bag on one of the bottom bunks and sit there quietly as the other girls talk eagerly about the ride we'll be going on this afternoon. I notice that I am the youngest kid there; everyone else looks to be around twelve or thirteen. I cling to the strap of my duffel bag and wonder if I will be able to call Mum if I get scared at night.

•

Later, at the stables, Ishani walks towards me leading the largest horse I have ever seen.

'This is Pablo,' she says. 'He is the biggest horse they have, but also the gentlest. He's a bit dopey, 'cause he's old. He'll just follow the other horses no matter what, so you'll be safe on him.'

She helps me put my foot into a stirrup and I hoist myself up and onto his back. He is wide like a barrel and he feels warm against my legs. He twitches his fur as the flies land on him, and I stroke his mane and neck and introduce myself to him.

It's a beautiful afternoon as Pablo follows the other kids on horses down a dirt track running alongside a wide river. The sun is low and golden and shines on the large gum trees lining the water's edge. Cicadas chirp and the air smells of lantana. Some of the kids are riding the horses bareback as they lead the horses into the water for a swim. Everyone looks so confident and I long to be able to ride a horse with such ease.

After an hour or so I start to relax; I no longer fear that Pablo might buck me off, and I release my grip on the saddle and sit comfortably holding the reins.

Dave trots past and gives me a wink. He's so charming. I blush and look away, and notice Shelley watching me.

'All the girls like him,' she says, 'and he likes all the girls . . . if you know what I mean.'

I don't really know what she means, but when I glance over at him I see him laughing as he touches one of the pretty girls on the shoulder. I wish he would wink at me again.

•

As the days pass, I start to understand what Shelley was talking about. Dave flirts with everyone. The girls giggle and talk about him when they think he's not listening, and steal looks at him when they think no one is watching. Shelley tells me he and Ishani have been kissing and doing 'other things' under the palms in front of the house when everyone is asleep. I feel a little pang of jealousy.

Meanwhile, I'm growing more confident on horseback. I've stopped wearing my boots and love the feeling of the stirrups on my bare feet. Every morning we train in a paddock. Dave holds the horse by a long rope and we ride around in wide circles learning how to trot, how to gallop. I raise my hips up to the top of the saddle with each of the horse's strides, learning the rhythm of how a horse moves and how you move with it.

'You're getting really good at riding,' says Dave. 'A natural, I reckon!'

I duck my head, pleased and embarrassed.

'Hey, I have an idea,' Dave continues. 'We have some wild Shetland ponies we need to break in, and you're the only one small enough to help us do it. Wanna have a go? I'll show you how it's done first, but you'll laugh 'cause my feet drag on the ground. I'm too tall!'

I agree, and a crowd of kids follow us to the paddock with the ponies to watch.

'You have to watch out for these ones,' Dave warns me. 'Shetland ponies love to bite!'

And sure enough, he goes to pat a pony and it whips its head around and bites his leg.

He yelps and looks at me, chortling, rubbing where the teeth got him. 'See? And they kick, too. Never walk behind one if you can help it; they're really quick to startle. Feisty buggers. Probably got small horse syndrome.'

The other kids laugh.

'So, how we break in any horse is simple really,' Dave explains. 'You take this rope and lasso it around the horse's neck, and then hop on its back as fast as you can and let it run for as long as it takes for it to calm down and stop. Then you can start training it. The trick is not to get bucked off. I'll do the first one while you watch, and then you can have a go.'

'Okay,' I say nervously.

Dave ropes one of the larger ponies and it rears up on its hind legs. As it comes back down, he climbs onto its back. He is right, though: he is way too tall for the small horse and his knees almost touch the ground.

The horse suddenly bolts out of the gate. Dave is simultaneously screaming and laughing. In a blur of spotty fur the horse runs about five hundred metres and then starts bucking violently until he finally dislodges Dave. At least he doesn't have far to fall.

Dave brushes himself off, then walks back over to us, limping slightly. 'Okay, Bertie—you're up. I'll catch one for you. Ya gotta be quick, though, mate. Once that rope is around its neck, just hop on its back and hold on for your bloody life!'

He approaches a small herd of ponies, who scatter in fright. He throws a rope high in the air and catches one. I quickly run up to it, throw my leg over its small back and grip the rope tightly in one hand.

And we're off!

The horse starts to run. Fast. But I am determined not to be thrown. I lean forwards and grasp hold of its mane. I can hear the others whooping and laughing in the distance but I barely take it in; I am completely focused on the horse. It rears and bucks but somehow I manage to stay on. Eventually, the horse comes to a stop and I hear everyone cheering.

I let go of the horse's mane but remember to keep a tight hold on the rope as I slide to the ground, glad to feel solid earth under my feet. The horse looks at me and then lowers it head to eat some grass. I feel so relieved I have survived without falling off, and the pony hasn't bitten or kicked me either.

Dave is running towards me. 'Mate!' he shouts breathlessly as he skids to a stop. 'Ya did good! No one has been able to break one of these guys for weeks!' His hand brushes mine for a second as he takes the rope.

He looks at me for a long moment with his blue eyes and my heart starts to pound, but we are interrupted by a ute pulling up nearby. Some older kids pile out of the back and come over to me, slapping my shoulders in congratulations. 'The Shetland queen!' they call me. It's obvious they are both surprised and impressed that I was able to stay on.

'She's got guts, that's for sure,' Dave agrees. As the others walk off, he says quietly, 'Maybe we can have a moment alone together later? After the bonfire?'

I nod quickly and look down, trying to act cool.

•

The flames of the bonfire rise up and lick the black sky.

I look up and follow the embers that fly and meet the stars in their own fizzy hot universe. It's like I'm seeing the scene from above, the other campers mere silhouettes against the glow of the fire.

One by one, everyone starts to leave. I linger by the fire, wondering when Dave and I might get our moment alone.

Suddenly I hear the sound of wheels spinning in mud. The camp ute is bogged.

'Righto!' says Dave, getting to his feet. 'Everyone get behind and push when I say so. Bertie hop in the front with me.'

Those of us left by the fire race over to help. My heart beats a little faster as I pull myself up into the cabin of the ute and lean back casually.

Dave opens the driver's-side door and slides behind the wheel. 'Push!' he shouts out the window, and then he glances across at me. He turns to the window again and shouts, 'C'mon, push!'

I look at him and then look away towards the lights of the old house, twinkling in the distance.

Suddenly I feel Dave's mouth on my cheek. His tongue is there too, and I start to turn towards him, but as I do he pulls away and leans out the window to urge everyone to keep pushing.

Then he turns his attention back to me. He kisses my cheek softly, his tongue moving on my skin. The world stands still and I wish the moment would never end.

There's a whoosh, and suddenly the car is freed from the mud and revving hard. A bunch of kids run up and hang off the windows and doors and I hear the thump of footsteps in the ute's tray.

'Alright, kiddos!' Dave shouts. 'We did it! Let's get back to camp.'

And just like that the spell is broken.

•

Back in our bunk beds, I tell Shelley that Dave kissed me.

'You like him, then?' she asks, surprised.

'Yeah, I like him,' I say shyly.

I wonder whether I will get to go under the palm trees with him in the night. Whether he might sneak into the shed tonight to get me. I watch the moon rise and fall through a crack in the curtains near my bunk, but he never shows up.

The next day Mum comes to pick me up. I overhear some of the other campers saying that Dave had sex with some of the younger girls, and he kissed pretty much everyone there. I wonder. Was sex like what I saw Dad and Victoria doing sometimes?

In the car Mum talks about what they have been up to back in the rainforest in Buderim. 'We've had a lovely time doing astrology readings and drinking dandelion tea. Your brother has been down at the kiln with Michael making pottery among the bamboo. He's made some beautiful things. How was camp?' she asks.

I look out the window for a moment, pondering the last few days. I want to tell her about the kiss, about Dave, but I decide not to. 'Well, I can ride bareback now and they taught me how to break in a Shetland pony!' I say.

'How wonderful!' she says, taking a hard right turn back up the steep hill home.

trinket

Trinket

Mum says I'm going to my aunty's house.

Garth has moved away, so I don't have to worry about seeing him.

I don't understand why my aunt would stay there after everyone found out about the horrible things Garth did, but she has. Maybe her cat Ponkie doesn't want to go . . . he does love to roll in those grey pebbles. Cats can be very persuasive.

As I walk up the drive to my aunt's place, I glance to my left. Garth's house has a For Sale sign on it. It feels empty. And eerie. I can see the front window, where his bedroom was. The mustard-yellow curtains are still there. The curtains that helped me escape into the sky with the birds. I shake my head to clear it of memories, but his breathing is loud in my ears.

Inside my aunty's house I still feel a little anxious. I sit on the couch and she brings me a cup of tea. It's hot and milky and tastes of honey.

'Would you like to listen to some XTC?' she asks.

I nod. Anything to replace the sound of breathing.

'Their album *Drums and Wires* has been remastered and it sounds amazing.'

She puts the disc in the CD player and presses play, and music explodes out of the speakers.

My aunt nods her head and plays air bass with her index and middle fingers, mouthing the words for 'Making Plans for Nigel'.

'Oh, just listen to that bass. I love the tone of Andy Partridge's voice. He's sooo sexy, don't you think?'

'Yeah, I like his voice,' I say. 'It reminds me of Peter Gabriel.'

She looks impressed.

'Hey, do you think I could have a look at your Fender bass again?' I ask, shouting slightly to be heard over the loud music. The last time I was here, Big Bertie showed me how to play 'slap' bass, and it was awesome. 'Talking bass', he called it.

'Oh, sure!' she says. She disappears into her bedroom and returns with a shiny, new-looking guitar case. She undoes the clasps, flips open the lid—and there it is. Polished and cherry red. The Fender bass. I just gaze at it for a while. The music still blares. I imagine the bassist from XTC playing this same guitar in front of a crowd of screaming fans. Maybe one day I'll own a bass like that.

My aunty turns the music down. 'You can have a go of it later, if you like.'

'That would be great, thank you,' I say.

'Now, I had organised for us to go and see Garth today, but he says today isn't good. He said he would like to talk to you on the phone instead, though, okay?'

I'm suddenly very queasy and my limbs feel like lead.

'Okay. Yes.' The words fall from my mouth like stones.

My aunty goes over to a side table and picks up a white cordless phone and dials a long number. I can hear the ringing from across the room. It feels like the walls shake with each *brrring brrrring.* It's louder than the music from before.

Then I hear his voice.

Ringing in my ears.

I watch my aunty's mouth move but I can't hear what she's saying and suddenly the phone is in my hand and I put it up to my ear.

'H-hello?' My voice cracks.

'Yes. Bertie.' Raspy, wheezy Garth is on the other end. 'I've been wanting to speak to you. I'm sorry you couldn't come and visit today, but maybe next time. I know Hamish would like to see you, too.'

I fidget and look out the window, avoiding my aunty's gaze. I can hear Hamish yapping in the background.

'You know, because of what you said, I have had to leave my whole life behind. My house, my neighbours, my friends. You know it was all you. You *liked* what I did. You *asked* for it. You *enjoyed* it. I only did what *you* wanted. Don't you ever forget that. It's all *your* fault. I've given your aunt a present for you—something to remind you of our time together. See you soon, I hope.'

The phone beeps in my ear. He is gone.

‘Now, Garth has asked me to give you this, but he said not to tell your mother.’ My aunty holds out a small red velvet pouch.

I take it from her and loosen the drawstring. Inside is a silver ring with a heart engraved on it and a little jewel that twinkles. I take it out and put it on my finger. It’s too big. I look at it and spin it around a few times with my fingers. I don’t know what to say. As I put it back into the velvet pouch I notice that there is a message etched in the inside of the band. *Love, G*, it reads in italics. I tuck the pouch into my pocket and decide I’ll keep it and I won’t tell.

‘Thank you,’ I say.

‘Don’t thank me, thank him. He gave me one, too,’ says my aunt.

Holyoake

After school one day, Mum announces that she has organised for Felix and me to go to something called Holyoake that evening.

'It's a type of support group for children with alcoholic fathers,' says Mum. 'You can share your stories with other children your own age. I think it might be good for you.'

'Sure, Mum,' we say.

I look at Felix and shrug, butterflies fluttering a little in my stomach.

We drive through peak-hour traffic to the other side of town. The sun is hot and golden, reflected in the windows of the cars that pass us. Flashes of light, a bit like the scales of fish swimming upstream. That's how it feels really—as if we are fighting the river's current, shoulder to shoulder, hoping that we make it. I look to the left and notice a giant bus depot. The buses are parked in neat rows like giant sardines in a can. If we are the fish swimming upstream, I wonder if the depot sardine can is our inevitable destination . . . to be licked up by the tongue of a giant cat. I can see our orange kombi tumbling up with the metal rattle tangle of the other cars, and the faces of me and Felix pressed against the window, wide-eyed as we are flung past the cat's fangs and swallowed down into its gullet. Travels in the gullet of a fluffy cat—our next adventure. I smile at this thought, and replay the scene again and again in my mind.

By the time we arrive the sun has set. We follow Mum into an old apartment block and up a set of stairs that goes on forever. On the top floor is a door with a piece of paper stuck on it that says: *Holyoake.*

We knock.

A friendly-looking middle-aged man opens the door. 'Hello,' he says. 'Can I help you?'

'Hi,' says Mum. 'I'm Genevieve de Couvreur, and I've brought my children for the group session—Felix and Bertie Blackman.'

'Yes! Please come in. Most of the kids are here already. But since we started this group a few weeks ago, we'll just need to do a quick interview with Felix and Bertie separately before we get started. Would that be okay, Genevieve? It's just routine for us.'

'Yes, yes, of course,' Mum says.

'Felix, why don't you come with me? Genevieve, you and Bertie can wait out here on these sofas. Tea and coffee and biscuits are in the kitchen to the left. You can help yourself. We won't be long.' The man leads Felix away.

I ask Mum if she wants something and she says no. I walk into the kitchen and find a jar of Arnott's biscuits. I can see my favourites—Kingstons—are buried at the bottom. Yum. I dig down and manage to extract two. Feeling pleased with myself, I walk back to the waiting area to see Mum fidgeting and looking out the window. I sit down. She looks at me eating my little prizes and smiles. 'We used to love eating Monte Carlos when we were little. We would eat the cream out from the middle and then eat the two biscuits separately so it would feel like double the treat.' I look down at my Kingstons with the chocolate centre and slowly eat them with relish. We don't have things like sweet biscuits at home. The only treats we're allowed are spelt licorice and the occasional coconut-covered apricot delight . . . and carob. Let's not forget the carob.

Before long Felix is back and it's my turn.

'Off you go,' says Mum. 'We will be waiting right here.' She smiles reassuringly.

I look at Felix and he looks happy enough, so I'm not too nervous, though the Kingston biscuits are rumbling around in my tummy, their sweetness making me feel a little ill.

I follow the man into a small office with a couple of armchairs and a desk in the corner. He gestures for me to sit in one of the chairs.

'Hello, Bertie, it's nice to meet you. My name is Simon.'

'Hi, Simon,' I say. I feel very small in the big chair.

'Now, this won't take long—I just have to ask you a few questions. These are just regular questions that we ask everyone who is new. Answer as honestly as you can; there's no wrong or right answer here.' He holds a pen in one hand and a pad of paper rests on his lap.

'Okay,' I say.

'Do you know what an alcoholic is?' he asks.

'Yes,' I say. 'That's what Dad is.'

'Okay, good. And do you think your mum is an alcoholic?'

'No. She's not like Dad,' I say.

'Has your mum or dad ever hit you?' Simon asks.

'Um . . . no.' I reply, looking away.

'Has anyone every touched you?' asked Simon.

'Yes, a man called Garth has. He did it a few times, but I told my mum about it. She said I wasn't the only one he did it to. Now we don't see him anymore.'

'I'm so sorry that happened to you, Bertie.' Simon says. 'Let me go and have a word with your mum? Don't worry. Everything is alright.'

Simon steps into the waiting area and walks over to Mum. He murmurs something, then ushers her into another room across the hall. I can see through the open door that Felix is sitting on one of the couches clutching a handful of biscuits. He looks bored.

My tummy churns as I shift in my chair.

A few minutes later Mum emerges from the other room and enters the office where I'm waiting. She is pale and quiet, and when she raises her hand to tuck a strand of hair behind her ear her bangles jangle on her wrist.

My ears start to ring.

She takes my hand and holds it tight.

I can hear Felix crunching on a biscuit out in the waiting room.

The room changes colour a bit as the light flickers. Blue and green and white flashes. My mother reaches for the telephone and starts dialling. I can hear her voice as she speaks into the telephone. I can hear Simon's voice nearby as he talks to someone else.

•

The next thing I know I am sitting in a circle with about eight other children. There is a young boy sitting near me and his mouth is moving but I can't make out what he is saying. It's like he's underwater. He opens his mouth and bubbles come out and float around the room. I decide to crawl inside each bubble to see if I can figure out what he is saying.

My dad is a gambler and he's drunk all the time.

My mum is always drunk or passed out on the floor.

My dad hits my mum. Sometimes there's blood.

Sometimes we don't eat for days.

I'm scared.

I'm alone.

I have to look after Mum when she vomits everywhere.

Nobody loves me but I love my mum and dad. They need me.

I feel like sometimes my own words are lost in bubbles. I can remember talking, but the sound is muffled and it feels like my tummy is full of rocks. The words float away from me but the feeling of them is still here. I can see everything going on around me, but it's happening in slow motion. Maybe that's to protect me from the thumps and crashes. I imagine the world the little boy lives in . . . his small flat and his drunk mother and his gambling father hitting the wall and throwing a bowl of cereal at his son. The boy being left for days on his own, starving. I wish I could take his pain away, but I don't know how.

I picture my own dad's home and him lying drunk, red-faced on the kitchen floor, Victoria remonstrating with him, as I watch it all unfold from afar, as if I don't really exist.

Past the bubbles and the words and the sounds, I can see light peeling in through the window. Behind the streetlight, the trees sway in the dark-blue night and there is the distant glow of the bus depot.

A bushy cat's tail flicks past the glass.

I wonder if the giant cat is going back for another sardine snack.

•

A few days later I hear Mum on the phone downstairs and she is shouting at Dad. She starts to cry. She asks him to stop crying. I hear my name. They are talking about me.

I look down and trace the lines of the wooden floorboards. I miss my dad.

Paper cigarettes

There's a new girl at school and her name is Natasha. I love her because she is different and wild and an outsider, just like me. When she laughs she sounds like a hysterical hyena and it makes me laugh too because that kind of feeling is contagious. I overhear kids in my class say that she is crazy, too crazy to be friends with, and that their parents would never let her come over to play. I don't understand that. She overhears them too sometimes and just laughs it off as if she doesn't care. This makes me like her even more.

One day Natasha tells me that her mum has a stall at Paddington Markets and I am excited because I know we will be going there on Saturday.

'My mum has friends who have stalls there,' I say. 'I'll come find you!'

•

That weekend the sun is shining and we are at the markets early, before it gets too hot. Circus flags are fluttering and New Age piano music swirls above the dense crowd of people. Felix and I duck and dive around all the long legs, racing past billowing multi-coloured silks, hessian fabrics, clanging wind chimes and buskers tossing flaming batons. But the bubble man is our favourite and we always race straight to his spot. He wears pink satin balloon pants and a top hat, but no shirt. He has a giant stick that he glides through the air, creating one giant bubble after another. Bubble within bubble. Universe within universe. When the sun shines on them I can see rainbows.

Suddenly I hear a familiar sound. The cackle of a human hyena. I whip my head around to see Natasha laughing and waving at me.

‘Come and see my mum’s stall,’ she calls. ‘We can get some money and go and get an ice cream!’

I dive back into the crowd and follow her.

Natasha’s mum is wearing a sequined cap and a leather bum bag, and she is as wide as her stall. When she sees us, she grins and puts down the necklace she has been making. ‘Oh good, Tasha, you’re back,’ she says to her daughter. ‘I need to go and get something to eat. Can you mind the stall?’

Natasha nods. ‘Sure, Mum. Don’t be long, though, Bertie and I wanna go get an ice cream.’

Beaded necklaces dangle from their stands and they make a nice sound as they blow in the breeze. There are blue necklaces and green necklaces, white and orange, but the ones I really like are those made in the colours of the Aboriginal flag—red, yellow and black. Natasha sees me staring at them.

‘Yeah, Mum makes those because I’m Aboriginal. She likes to celebrate it. Cool, huh? I’ll steal one for you, if you want.’

‘Nah,’ I say. ‘She’ll notice if I’m wearing one all of a sudden. Maybe I can save up my pocket money and buy one some day.’

Natasha shrugs and grabs a necklace hanging close to her face and shoves it in her pocket. Then she takes a bunch of gold coins from her mum's purse. She giggles. 'Why don't you come over later, after the market? I've got a bubble-maker like the man in the pink pants, and I've got Barbies too. You could stay the night and come with us to this big festival for my people tomorrow.'

'Okay!' I say. 'I'll ask my mum to drop me round.'

•

Natasha's house is near where Dad lives but down the other end of the park, near where the storm water drains are. When they are full, they stink like the toilet, but when they are empty you can take your bike or skateboard down and ride around, like it's a giant skate park.

Mum drops me off out the front of the house and I run up the path and bang on the door.

Natasha must have been waiting for me, because she immediately flings it open.

'Come in!' she says, wide eyed. 'Mum is in bed working, so we can just do whatever we want. Let's go play in my room.'

As I follow her into the house, I notice that it is stacked floor to ceiling with newspapers, furniture and what looks like piles of junk. There's so much stuff we have to squeeze through gaps to get past it. You can barely walk in a straight line. It's dark, too, and there's a smell of damp mixed with reheated food.

'Natasha? . . . NATASHA!' comes a shout from the other side of the house.

Natasha ignores it.

'NATASHA!'

'WHAT?' Natasha bellows. 'Bertie just got here! We're going to go play. We'll want a bucket of KFC for dinner, okay?'

I can hear distant mumbling and shuffling and then silence.

Natasha doesn't seem to care, and she strides on impatiently. Natasha's bedroom is much the same as the rest of the house; it's crammed with piles of things, and straining at the seams. She pulls a pile of dolls from under her bed.

'I used to have Barbie clothes, but I can't find them anymore. Anyway, she's better off without them.'

We put Barbie and Ken into a large pink car and push them around in it.

'Fuck this,' Natasha says after a while. 'Let's smoke some paper.'

She rummages around in the mess for a few minutes then produces a box of matches and a small notepad. She rips a piece of paper from it, rolls it into a neat tube and twists the end. We go to stand by the window.

'You smoked before?' Natasha asks.

'Yeah,' I say. 'In Buderim. Come on, let's light it.'

Natasha strikes a match and lights the end of the paper. She inhales quickly and then starts to cough, grimacing. 'Ugh. That shit burns. Here—your turn.'

I take the paper cigarette and put it in my mouth. It's soggy where Natasha sucked on it. She lights a match and raises it to the end. I inhale and a searing pain shoots down into my lungs. 'AGH! That does burn!' I splutter. But I take another drag anyway.

Suddenly, Natasha's mum bursts into the room.

'Oh, *Natasha*! Not *again*! What did I tell you? You're too young to smoke! Now go outside and get some fresh air. Go and play outside!'

Natasha giggles and scampers up, and I follow her, looking down at the ground, too scared to make eye contact with her fuming mother. We run out the back door, through the garden and climb over the back fence into the laneway behind her house.

'Let's go down into the stormwater drains,' I suggest. 'I think it's low tide. We can play chicken in the pipes.'

We run down the laneway, jump a low fence and climb down to the canal. It's mostly dry apart from long trails of slimy water that lead into two large dark pipes. We stand side by side and gaze into the openings—it's like looking into the ends of a giant set of binoculars, or those big open clown mouths at the Easter show.

I look at Natasha. 'Let's run into the pipes and see who can go the furthest before they get chicken. The one who stays in the dark longest wins.'

We kick off at top speed; I go into one pipe and Natasha goes into the other. I can hear her giggling and the light sploshing of puddles. Our footsteps splash in wonderful synchronicity. All of a sudden I feel panicked and stop. The darkness feels so deep and black. I put my hand out in front of me and my hand disappears into the black like it's passed through some kind of veil. I look down and I cannot see my body at all . . . It's like I am invisible.

My heart starts to pound.

I turn to face the white glow of the afternoon we left behind. My skin picks up the hue and suddenly I am real again. It scares me that the dark can be so hungry.

I bolt back towards the tunnel opening faster than I entered, the air whooshing in my ears and the water splashing up the back of my legs.

When I burst out into the daylight I see Natasha has already made her way back and is sitting on the fence looking at me grinning, and giggling under her breath. Neither of us mentions the deep dark.

Keen to leave the tunnels behind, I say, 'Let's go up to Franklins. I've got three dollars twenty in my pocket, and we can get a snack.' I feel the coins jangle as they hit my leg, ready to be spent.

We walk up the street to the supermarket and I go straight to the underwear section. I'm longing to buy a white Chesty Bond singlet. I've seen the boys at school wearing them with shorts and I want to look like them.

But the singlets are eight dollars. Disappointed, I look at my handful of change. I could keep saving . . . or I could steal it. I look around; there's no one else in the aisle. I break out in a little sweat and start to reach out a trembling hand . . .

Suddenly Natasha skids around the corner and runs up to me. 'Why are you looking at singlets, you weirdo?' she says. 'Let's go get some yoghurt—we can throw it at cars in the car park.'

I tuck away my feelings of wanting to dress like a boy and save them for another quiet moment.

We run to the dairy section and grab a few cheap tubs of yoghurt, then carry them out to the car park and look around to see if anyone is looking, but no one is there. To our delight, we spot a convertible with its top down. 'That one!' I say.

We each peel the top off a tub of yoghurt and run towards the car. We pour yoghurt all over the front seats and then I throw my tub at the windscreen, where it explodes in a gooey mess. We take off down the street back to Natasha's place before anyone can see us, laughing so hard we can barely run. The light of the day has disappeared now and we need to get home before it's too late.

Approaching Natasha's house, we can see a big shadow looming by the gate with hands on hips.

It's Natasha's mum. She is a big woman anyway, but in her fury she seems even bigger. Her chest is heaving in anger. 'Natasha!' she shouts. 'You bloody shit, you've been gone for hours. Bertie's mum might have called and I had no idea where you were.'

We skid to a stop about a metre away. I look down at the ground, too frightened to make eye contact. But Natasha is unconcerned. 'Oh, Mum, just go back to bed and bead some more necklaces. We can take care of ourselves.'

She pushes past her mum—who tries to grab her, but Natasha is too quick—and enters the house, with me trailing behind. We go into Natasha's bedroom and she locks the door. 'I guess that means no dinner for us,' says Natasha. 'Let's just go to bed. There'll be heaps of nice food at the festival tomorrow, and music too, and you can meet some of my mob. Yothu Yindi is gonna be playing.'

'Cool!' I say. 'I love Yothu Yindi.'

That night my tummy grumbles as I dream of dark tunnels, the rising water, and the blackness enveloping me inch by inch.

•

When I wake up the next morning I'm alone in the bedroom. I walk out to the kitchen and find Natasha eating a bowl of Weet-Bix.

'C'mon, sleepyhead, ya better get dressed. We're going to the festival and it's a long drive.'

She follows me back to her room, where I stand and look in the mirror, unhappy with how boring my clothes are compared to Natasha's.

'Can I borrow something to wear?' I ask. 'I want to look like you today.'

'Sure!' says Natasha. She opens her enormous wardrobe, which is crammed with clothes and shoes and old, faded toys.

I rummage around and grab a pair of ski boots and a T-shirt with the Aboriginal flag on it.

Natasha tosses me some pink leggings. 'And these!' She scoops up some necklaces of red, black and yellow beads from the top of her dresser. 'These too.'

I put them all on and am pretty pleased, shifting my feet inside the too-big boots. I look at myself in the mirror. I look perfect.

Natasha's mum walks in and shakes her head. 'You kids are crazy. Come on then, you nut bags—let's go.'

The festival is in a massive park and it takes ages to get there. When we get out of the car, I see that a lot of other people are wearing red, black and yellow, too—it makes me feel good to know we're all dressed the same.

'C'mon, let's go see the band,' Natasha says. She grabs my hand and we run towards the stage, and are immediately swept up in a big dancing crowd.

Yothu Yindi is playing 'Treaty', and everyone around me looks happy and determined as they clap their hands in the air, and smile and point at me and Natasha holding hands and dancing alongside them. I smile back. For the first time in a long while I feel like I belong. Like I'm not an outsider looking in. Like I'm not on a cloud looking down. I look down at Natasha's hand in mine and wish that this moment could last forever.

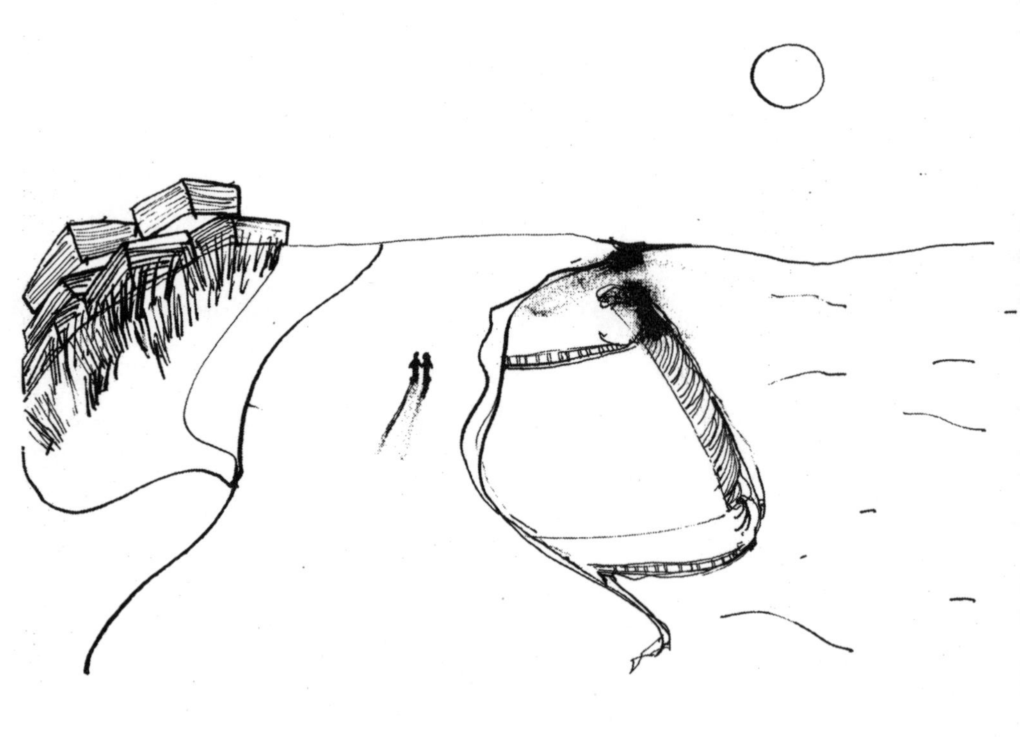

Bundeena

I have this recurring dream.

I am on the beach at Bundeena, lying on a steep dune, and the sand beneath me is hard and wet and cold. I try to lift my head but I don't have the strength. It's like the sand particles are made of magnets, holding my limbs down. Their grip is tight but invisible.

The top of the dune is covered in long green-grey grass. Terracotta rooftops peer over the top. The sea laps gently at the shore below—but it's more like a lake than the ocean. Flat and glassy. Placid. The water rises towards me in thin streams, like long ladders, but when I reach out to touch them, they recede, like the inquisitive feelers of a snail retracting into its soft body.

The sun is shining, a light so white it is dazzling. I rub my eyes but when I open them again the light is still so bright and searing that it blinds me and my eyes start to water. I press my fingers hard into my eye sockets in frustration, hoping to relieve the pressure. Then I am plunged into black—relief for a moment. Coming into soft focus, red Chinese dragons furl and curl around each other, their wings and scales flapping in mid-air like kites. They are gentle and stay in their world, watching.

I squint hard through the tears and see the beach. Two long shadows stretch across the sand and I realise that they belong to a couple strolling hand in hand. Their backs are to me as they walk casually away.

And then I am standing at the top of the stairs near my bedroom. I look down.

The dream comes to me, and the blinding, burning light makes me grit my teeth. I shake my head to get rid of it, but the clenching feels good, so I lean into the feeling of it. I feel a sense of relief, like I'm scratching a really deep itch. I bite down harder. And harder. My limbs are full of this rising tide but they are sinking, heavy as lead, and they yearn to feel tight like my gritted teeth. Like the feeling is a new superpower that I don't yet know how to wield. I have to do something to release the energy, release the need.

The stairs come towards me.

I feel my body hit the scratchy carpet, feel the edge of the step.

I grit my teeth harder and clench my jaw and bite the inside of my lip.

And then I am tumbling.

I hit the concrete wall at the bottom of the stairs. The impact hugs me tight.

The echo of my fall follows me as I get up and run back to the top.

I throw myself down again.

My teeth clatter and my knees are grazed, but the shadows and hands and eyes that haunt me feel further away. Finally. The falling feels good. This feeling I want. This feeling I like. I can't get enough. Again and again I run back up to the top of the stairs and throw myself down. The thumping of my body becoming an addictive tempo. Drum fills, body spills, it's all the same. I can hear Mum's jangling bangles all the way downstairs, as she turns up the volume to 'Sweet Dreams' by the Eurythmics and her footsteps walk back into the kitchen to continue her phone call. It's the perfect accompaniment to my silent percussion above.

Driving south

I love the winding roads that peel down the final stretch of highway towards the coast south of Sydney. There's a tapestry that hangs above Dad's bed, full of mazes and secret gardens, and it reminds me of this scene, the feeling of it—like you could fall off the edge any minute. The angles. The giant ferns. The dark green bush pressing up against the white lines that mark the borders of the road, keeping us hugged in there. The big blue ocean in the distance merging against the sky in a long streaky line.

I'm in the car with my niece Clementine and her mum Kimberly, who is Mum's best friend. We are going to their family holiday house for the weekend. I like driving with them because Kimberly has a really good stereo in the car and the music is always loud, plus the wide leather seats feel nice.

A deep voice, soft but powerful, bellows out of the dashboard speakers. I get chills. The tone wraps around me.

'Who's this singing?' I ask.

'Oh, it's Nick Cave,' Kimberly replies. 'Isn't he just amazing?' Her long fingers tap the steering wheel and her steely gaze looks off beyond the moment.

I've never heard anything like it. I have noticed that when I listen to music lately, I feel it in places I've never felt before. It's like the sound has pushed through to something deeper in me. Deeper than my skin, deeper than my blood, into something I can't see. I can't even see it when I shut my eyes. It hums, and spatters, and coos and reverberates and clatters around. Like the sound has found an internal kitchen and it's cooking up a secret storm.

Words of sailing ships and burning bridges, his voice sinks into my bones. I feel like where he reaches, I could also reach. I want to write like this. I want to make something like this. I want to be a sound like this . . . that oozes into a human soul and paints its own new landscape. It's more than what I imagine when I'm reading a storybook. To make sounds that paint worlds . . . vast, and invisible to the human eye. A place to fall into. I can feel it tugging on me. This is what I must do. This is who I am.

Words of being held tight in arms as the world comes crashing down. The drums kick in. They kick my heart awake.

I think about the moments that have filled the void in time since I told Mum about Garth and what happened to me. The closed doors at home turn into the piano. Mum's voice, quiet and upset, turns into the guitars. My insides, squirming and trying to find a safe place to be in my skin, knowing that only in stillness can I feel secure, crawl in between the notes.

Bells cascade over the deep voice, and the words turn into the vast world that is still gliding past the car windows. Down the road like a snaky shape, I'm watching our reflections in the window and these moments are all in the past already as the music reaches forwards, and time stands still.

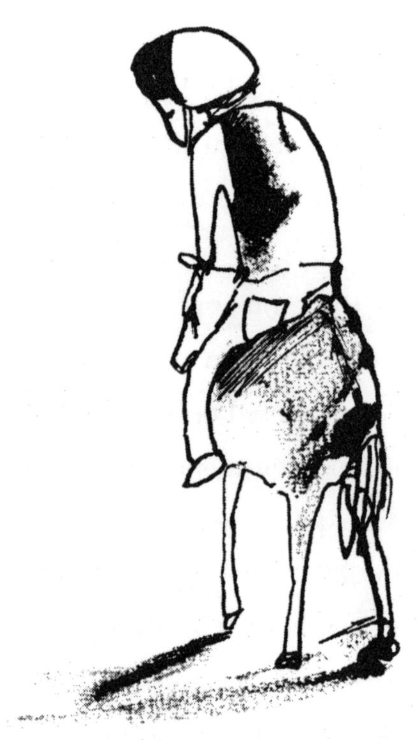

Rodeo rider

My oldest friend is Emma Lou. Her mum Bella used to babysit my mum when Mum was a little girl. They often tell stories of when they lived in Mosman, and Bella's father had a butcher shop called Lamb's Butcher that was down the end of their street. Lamb is their last name and I think it's the perfect name for a butcher. A bit like the vet near us who's called Dr Cat.

Bella also has a son, Luke, who's older than me. I like Luke a lot. He's got scruffy blond hair and he wears hypercolour t-shirts and rides BMX bikes. They have moved around a lot over the years—usually to different properties to manage farms or horses—but now they are living up in Katherine, in the Northern Territory, and Mum is sending me up there for the winter holidays. It's rodeo season, and the Lambs usually go on tour with their horses.

Luke picks me up from the airport in Darwin. The last time I saw him he was a young boy, but now he is a big teenager with a deep voice and a mop of bleached hair with black roots.

'Hey, Bertie. I wasn't sure if you'd remember what I looked like, but I remember you! You haven't changed much. You're still small.' He chuckles. 'We'll drive out to Katherine tomorrow, but tonight you'll be staying here in Darwin with me and Dad. I can show you around this arvo. Darwin's got a great beach—almost as cool as Sydney.'

I look at Luke's bleached hair and wish my hair was like that rather than a short brown bob. 'How did you get your hair that colour?' I ask.

'Peroxide, mate. Got a bottle from the chemist and just poured it on. Easy as.'

Luke takes me for a walk around the centre of town and then we go down to the beach for a swim. It's low tide and the shallows go on for a long way before it's deep enough to dive in. Luke dives under a small wave and shakes his head in the air. He tells me about the swimming carnivals he's competed in at school. I look at his broad shoulders and muscly chest. 'Sometimes there's good surf here, too.' He ducks under another wave.

That night we have takeaway pizza for dinner in their small apartment, and then I lie on the couch in a sleeping bag and listen to the sounds of the city floating in through the open window. Fluorescent streetlights flicker outside. Impatient for morning, I watch the clock until eventually I fall asleep.

•

As soon as we reach the city's outskirts the red earth starts to creep up on the concrete, until the concrete is gone and the city is too and it is just vast red desert. I always thought the desert would have no trees, but there are clutches of gum trees and shrubs and long branches that stick out of the earth like otherworldly creatures gasping for air. Frozen in time.

We don't talk much on the drive. I think about my friend Natasha. She says her dad is from up here, but he's a missionary and she doesn't know where he is at the moment. I wonder what he might look like; I picture a man in an old suit with his back turned, standing under a washing line, sheets billowing in the wind.

We get to Katherine a few hours later, driving across a bridge over a wide dry riverbed. I notice small clusters of people gathered under shady trees. 'That's how the locals keep cool,' Luke's dad says. I think about the festival I went to in Sydney recently with Natasha, and how good it felt to be part of that community, even just for one night. I wish I could come and live up here and hang out under the gum trees. It seems like the most natural thing in the world to do. I look at the freckly skin on my arms and pinch it. I don't like my white skin. I wonder if I would feel different in a new skin. A skin that had different secrets maybe.

We pull up to their house in a haze of red dirt. It's raised up on stilts and there are old bikes underneath. Bella and Emma Lou come down to greet us and I feel shy but excited to have finally arrived.

'It's fireworks night tonight,' Emma Lou tells me. 'Everyone comes out front with garbage bins full of fireworks and lets them off all down the street. It's the only place left in Australia where it's still legal; ya can't do this in Sydney. We only have a small pile of 'em, but the neighbours have bigger stashes.'

I look at Emma Lou. She has grown heaps since I last saw her. She has longer hair than me, shaved underneath, and she is wearing a cut-off t-shirt. She looks tough and strong.

•

That afternoon we go for a bike ride. We cycle down the long wide streets dotted with suburban houses. Emma Lou can do wheelies and stunts but all I can do is try my best to keep up with her, puffing with the effort. Emma laughs at me as I cautiously brake a few times, the wheels moaning and jarring underneath me, almost in a mocking way. She manoeuvres around with such ease and confidence. We ride into the desert and skid around some piles of old wrecked cars. I feel like I'm on a different planet, far away from anything I've ever known.

Later, when the sun starts to go down, we walk around and watch all the fireworks going off down the street. Smoke haze and sparks flint and crack as the red sunset morphs from the colour of the earth to the inky black of the starry night sky.

All the kids from up and down the street run around together, hooting and shouting with excitement, as the adults stand in small groups, talking and sipping from their stubbie holders.

Afterwards, I unroll my sleeping bag on the floor of Emma Lou's room and we talk until we fall asleep. In the middle of the night I wake up and need to do a wee. I wait and wait, because I'm scared of the dark and I don't want to get up, until I can't hold on any longer. I go into the bathroom and am about to sit on the toilet when I see there's a huge toad sitting in the bowl. I consider peeing on the toad, but I picture it trying to jump up into my bum. I decide to wee in the sink instead.

•

The next morning we wake up early and hit the road, heading to the Adelaide River rodeo. Chex, the family's lovely big brown horse, is being towed in a horse trailer.

'You're in for a real treat, Bertie,' Bella says. 'You and Em will get to go mutton busting, and we'll sleep outside in swags overnight with the rest of the show folk—you'll have a real country experience! Then after Adelaide River, we'll go up to Tipperary Station and stay there a few nights. It's one of the biggest cattle stations in the Territory; they use helicopters to herd the cattle. And they have an amazing zoo, too, with giraffes and everything.'

'Oh wow!' I say excitedly. 'Well, I've slept outside a few times, but never in a swag.'

We arrive in Adelaide River and drive up the back of the showground to set up camp. Emma Lou goes into the horse trailer to bring Chex out, then hands me the lead.

'Here you go. Take Chex over there and tie him to that pole so he can eat his lunch.'

I take hold of the rope and lead the big horse down the metal ramp. I am nervous leading such a big animal and the adrenaline makes my heart beat fast. I can feel his hooves whipping the air right near my feet and I worry he might step on me but he doesn't. I tie him up and feed him an apple.

Emma Lou and I take off to go on some carnival rides while Bella enters Chex into the show. We ride quad bikes around and around through a muddy maze. I can smell the wet mud flicking up the back of my legs. The young guys manning the ride are pointing at me and laughing and I notice Emma Lou is too. I don't know why.

In the afternoon, it's time for the mutton busting. I look at all the kids sitting on the fence behind the arena. They are wearing cowboy hats and checked shirts. I look down at my blue surfie singlet and city jeans and feel quite out of place. They all seem so tough compared to me.

The marshals give us each a number and tell us to wait to be called.

Finally I hear a marshal call, 'Number eight!' It's my turn.

I walk out onto the centre of the small arena and see that, instead of a sheep, I'll be riding a goat.

'They ran out of sheep this year. Goats are just as fun, though.' The marshal winks at me. 'Now all you have to do is hold on to this rope and try not to get bucked off. Can ya do that?'

'Yeah,' I say, though I'm feeling a bit uncertain.

I'm helped up onto the bare back of the goat; its fur twitches from the flies.

'Three . . . two . . . one . . . go!'

I am flung out of the gate and the goat is running at top speed. I hang on as tight as I can but it bucks furiously and it feels like I am only on it for a few seconds before I'm suddenly on my back on the dirt.

Emma jogs over to me. 'Ya did alright,' she says with a grin as she helps me to my feet. 'Almost stayed on as long as me.'

I feel a bit tougher now that I've been bucked off a wild goat in a rodeo, and I'm especially taken with the red trucker hat they gave me as a prize. I've always wanted a trucker hat. I can't wait to tell Mum about it.

We stand back behind the gates and watch the adults ride the bulls and wild horses. I am in awe of the strength of the animals and how dangerous and wild the rodeo is.

Back by the horse chute, I walk around in my jeans and red hat with no shirt on and feel like I've become one of them. A rodeo rider. The smell of the horses and the mud and the smoke from the small campfires wafts through the air. I lie on my swag and look at the sky, with a twig in my mouth.

•

As we're leaving Adelaide River the next day, I ask Bella if she can make my hair like Luke's.

'Yeah, I reckon we can do that,' she says. 'Your mum might get a bit of a surprise, though! We can get a bottle of peroxide from the chemist, and when we are up in Tipperary I can pour some on your hair and see what colour it goes. It's hard to say what'll happen; your hair is pretty dark.'

It's only an hour or so later that we drive in through the gates of Tipperary Station, past the enormous zoo. From the car I can see zebras and the long necks of giraffes. As we near the big house, dogs run up to the car, barking, and Bella's friends come out to meet us. There are some more kids our age, too. They are carrying whips. Emma Lou takes one and cracks it. She looks at me. 'Wanna try?'

I take the leather whip in my hand and flick it up, then slam it down hard, trying to make it crack, but it makes no sound at all and I just feel very awkward. All the other kids laugh at me. 'Let's make some smaller whips,' Emma says kindly. 'They might be easier for you to crack.'

We spend all afternoon plaiting black rope and fashioning some handles from old sticks. My whip is much smaller than the big leather one, and I mimic the other kids' gestures until finally I hear an almighty *crack*!

Everyone stops and looks at me, impressed.

The others put down their whips and head to the pool to cool off, but I stay behind to get my hair done.

Bella pours capfuls of peroxide over my head. The smell of ammonia makes me gag and my eyes are stinging, but I don't care—I'm excited to have bleached-blonde hair like Luke's.

Then I hear Emma say, 'Mum, it's made her hair orange!'

Bella tells me to go inside and wash my hair. When I'm done, I look in the mirror. Emma Lou was right: my hair is as orange as a carrot. Bella had told me we could only do one bottle because too much peroxide might make all my hair fall out. I guess orange will have to do.

I run outside and dive into the pool. The cold water is a relief from the sweltering heat and it soothes my burning scalp. I open my eyes underwater and see the spinning legs of the other kids as they jump in and out, playing tip. For some reason I have the sense I could stay down here forever without taking a breath. I swim down deeper until I'm sitting on the bottom of the pool next to a couple of toy cars that must have been thrown in. I look up and the sun is glittering through the ripples on the surface. Out of the corner of my eye I can see strands of my orange hair floating in the water.

•

On the plane home I look out the window at the red desert getting smaller and smaller. My whip sticks out of the seat pocket in front of me and my trucker hat feels heavy and good on my head. I feel taller and stronger.

At the airport in Sydney, Mum screeches when she sees me. 'Your hair! What happened to your hair?'

'The sun bleached it,' I say. 'And then it turned the colour of the desert. It's magic out there.'

The dog and the witch

Everyone at school thinks my friend Olivia's grandmother is a witch. She has all the characteristics of a witch: big knobbly nose; long, greasy, silver hair; loose flowing clothes; gnarled hands; hunched back. And she lives with Olivia and Olivia's mother in a dark crumbling old terrace on Cleveland Street, a rather down-at-heel main thoroughfare, which seems to me exactly the kind of place a modern witch would live if she were trying to pass for 'normal'. I am fascinated by her; I often think of Roald Dahl's description of a witch and see if I can detect the symptoms of wig rash or spot her square toes. The younger children scream and run when she comes into the school grounds, but I am in year six now, so I just lean against the wall nonchalantly and watch the chaos unfold.

One day, Olivia invites me over to her house after school. Olivia has always kept to herself, but I think she's pretty cool so I accept, secretly hoping to find out for sure whether her grandmother is indeed a witch. Even though I feel pretty mature, being almost a high schooler, I approach the front door of Olivia's house with the trepidation of my younger self. I gaze at the drawn curtains of the front window and wonder whether Olivia's grandmother is casting spells inside.

Olivia unlocks the door and we walk down the hall, floorboards creaking, to a cluttered living room full of worn furniture. Olivia chucks her schoolbag on the floor and calls, 'Mu-u-um?'

'Yes, Olivia?' a voice bellows from upstairs.

'I'm home. My friend Bertie from school has come over to hang out.'

Footsteps thump down the stairs and Olivia's mothers leans over the banister. 'Hi, Bertie. Nice to meet you. You girls need anything?'

‘Nah,’ Olivia says. ‘We’ll just hang in my room.’

A scruffy white dog runs to me and scratches at my shoes. I pat him and he seems excited and grateful for the attention.

‘Rodger!’ Olivia says. ‘Stop annoying my friend!’

Chastened, Rodger scurries up the stairs out of sight, his long claws scratching and slipping on the wood.

We walk upstairs to Olivia’s room. Compared to my room, it’s massive. Two French doors open onto a balcony overlooking the street and there’s a double bed pushed against one wall. (I only have a single bed.) There are band posters on the walls—some falling down where old blu-tack is coming unstuck—and a dresser with a huge mirror, long necklaces draped over one corner. Rodger the dog is nestled in a pile of clothes on the floor, scratching himself.

The peeling paint on the walls flap in a sudden gust of breeze as Olivia thrusts open the doors to the balcony, letting in the long honks of the trucks whizzing up the main road.

I stare at a poster of Kurt Cobain as Olivia mists the room with one of her many cans of Impulse spray deodorant. The scent gets caught in the back of my throat. All the girls at school have started to wear it but I think it stinks.

Olivia sits beside me on the bed.

She looks a little nervous. 'I asked you to come over because I'm in trouble and I need your help,' she says in a low voice.

I look at her anxiously. 'What is it?' I ask. 'Are you okay?'

'I got into this gang recently, and they have eyes everywhere. They can even see me right now.' Olivia looks around the room slowly, eyes wide. Then she looks at me. 'They have told me that I have to kiss you.'

I scan the room for spy cameras, but there is nothing obvious.

'Really?' I say. 'Are you sure? It would be pretty hard for them to see what you were doing in here without a secret camera or whatever.' I look into Kurt Cobain's big blue eyes to make sure they aren't moving.

'Well they can. They told me they have ways of watching. They said if we don't kiss, then they will bash me.'

I consider this. I don't want her to get bashed, but I don't want to kiss her either. Frankly, her story doesn't seem that believable.

'Nah, I don't want to kiss you,' I say.

Olivia sighs. 'Well, if you won't kiss me, then . . . Rodger! Come here, Rodger! C'mon, boy!' Olivia slaps her knees.

The dog comes bounding over.

'Lie down, Roger!' she orders.

To my horror, she bends down and starts to touch her dog's penis. I shriek in disgust. 'No! Don't. That's so wrong!' I stand up and start to back away.

She laughs. 'Kiss me or I'll rub his stuff on you!' She holds up her hand and I see white goo on her fingertips.

She lunges at me and I manage to swerve out of the way. I bolt out of the bedroom and seek refuge in the bathroom. I slam the door shut and lock it. 'Fuck off!' I call. 'Get away from me!'

Olivia bangs on the bathroom door, hooting with laughter.

Suddenly I hear Olivia's mother shout, 'Olivia, shut up! I'm trying to have a nap. Go to the park if you want to run around instead of thumping all over the house like a herd of elephants.'

I sit very still against the cold dirty tiles and wait for silence to descend. Eventually, when I've heard nothing for a few minutes, I open the door and stick my head. The coast is clear. I return to Olivia's room and see her lying on the bed, flicking the pages of a magazine.

'I'm gonna go,' I say.

She looks up at me. 'Already? Okay. I'll walk you out.'

I look carefully at her hands and they look clean. I breathe a little sigh of relief and relax a bit. We walk back downstairs and I see Olivia's grandmother in the kitchen adjoining the living room. I quickly snatch up my backpack and steal a glance at her as she stirs sugar into a hot cup of tea.

'Hello, dear,' she says with a tiny grin. She lifts a hand to scratch her head and I could swear I see the hairline move. As I suspected: it's a wig.

I walk outside onto Cleveland Street and sit on the hot brick wall, waiting for my mum to pick me up, hoping she won't be late.

The party

Not long after the afternoon when I went to her house, Olivia invites me to go with her to a party in Maroubra. 'My mum lets me go wherever I want as long as she can drop me off and pick me up. Just tell your mum you're staying the night at mine. If your mum calls, my mum will just lie and say we're at the movies or whatever.'

I wonder briefly how Olivia's mother can be so casual about where she goes, and then I remember how weird it was at their house and just presume she doesn't really care what her daughter does. I'm not sure

I want to go to a party with Olivia, but I'm a bit scared of her after what happened with the dog, so I say yes.

•

On the afternoon of the party, Olivia's mum picks us up after school in an old pale blue VW beetle. You can hear the spluttering engine from a block away. We slide into the back seat; we've already changed into our clothes for the party in the toilets inside.

'Now I want you girls to be careful,' Olivia's mother lectures us. 'No doubt there will be older boys at this party, and you know what they're like. I don't mind if you drink, but just be sure to take care of each other.'

It's a hot afternoon and the vinyl of the seat is sticking to skin. I'm a little nervous, but I play it cool, just staying quiet and looking out the window.

The car wheezes to a halt outside a big house on a wide suburban street.

'Thanks, Mum,' says Olivia. 'Can you pick us up at, like, nine tomorrow morning?'

'Sure thing,' says her mum. 'Here's twenty dollars to get some dinner for yourselves.'

I follow Olivia across the road to a park.

'We can just hang here till the sun goes down,' Olivia says. 'I like to get where I'm going early so I can smoke some ciggies.'

We sit on the swings and Olivia pulls out a packet of Peter Stuyvesant. 'Want one?' she asks.

'Yeah, okay,' I say.

I accept one, light it and take a short drag. The smoke hits the back of my throat and I cough a bit.

Olivia laughs. 'I didn't think you smoked,' she says.

'Maybe I should start,' I say with a shrug. I take another short drag, bum-puffing out of fear I might choke again.

We stay on the swings and watch the sun sink behind the the rusty fences that line the park. I look over at Olivia. She's wearing a short, pleated tartan skirt, scummy Converse sneakers and an old white t-shirt that's a bit ripped. Her messy long blonde hair is flicked over her shoulders. I gaze at my oversized jeans and old Hot Tuna t-shirt and suddenly feel very young compared to her. I haven't gone through puberty yet like some of the other girls. I can still swim at the beach without a top. I even get mistaken for a boy still, which I like.

There's a blast of loud rap music from the house across the road and Olivia stands up. 'I'm gonna get stoned tonight,' she says. 'I reckon there will be heaps of drugs at the party. C'mon, let's go in.'

We cross the road and tap on the front door of the large house. A lanky teenage guy opens it. 'Oh, hey, Olivia. Wassup?'

I follow Olivia inside. The house is already full of people. Teenagers sitting on the kitchen island, others smoking bongs on the beige leather couches with *Video Hits* blaring on an oversized big-screen TV. We are a lot younger than everyone else there.

Then a boy who looks to be more our age comes over. 'Yo, girls! I'm Aiden.'

'Hi, Aiden,' says Olivia. 'You're Jared's little brother, right? Do you know where he is?'

'Yeah, they're all out the back. You guys want a drink?'

'Nah,' says Olivia. 'I'd like some weed, though.'

'Sweet. The boys will sort you out with that,' says Aiden.

'I'll have a drink,' I say quickly. 'I've never been drunk before.'

Aiden pours some vodka into a couple of glasses and adds a splash of Coke. 'I'll get ya drunk,' he says, chuckling, and hands me one of the glasses.

I take a big sip and notice him watching me.

'Good, eh?' he says. 'Okay, come with me.'

We follow him along a narrow hallway to the back deck. There's a large spa there, and some guys with shaved heads are sitting around the edge, dangling their legs in the water. They are all laughing and watching a couple of girls in bikinis sauntering towards them.

Someone hands Olivia a bong and she takes a big drag. I can hear the water bubbling and the low hiss of air through the cone. I raise my glass to have another sip but realise it's empty.

'Ya want another?' Aiden says.

I nod. 'Yeah, cool, thanks,' I say.

As Aiden walks off, Olivia says, 'Be careful of him.'

'Why?' I ask. 'He looks like he's about eleven or twelve, like us. He can't be that dangerous.' I shrug and cough a bit from the smoky haze that's surrounding Olivia.

The older guys by the spa have taken an interest in her now and, realising this, she sticks her chest out and laughs, flicking her hair in a flirty way. I wouldn't even know how to flirt like that. I still feel like a kid. I try to flick my hair but I just feel awkward. My hair's too short to flick anyway. I put my hands in my pockets and start to feel warm and a bit dizzy. But I'm more relaxed, too; a little more confident and at ease.

Everything becomes blurry after that.

I'm in the spa and a guy with a shaved head and tattoos moves close to me. The music feels warped and it's like I'm playing the part of myself in a teen movie. The vodka and Cokes keep coming and suddenly I'm back in the park, sitting on a swing. Aiden is next to me and he leans over and kisses me. My first kiss from a boy my own age.

'Getting drunk is fun, hey?' he slurs. 'Do you want to go upstairs?'

I hear myself answer and then I'm following him as he leads me by the hand back through the heaving party. I can hear Olivia's laugh. 'Hey, Bertie! Where you going?' she shouts, but she's out of sight before I can respond.

It's dark and Aiden is kissing me. He puts his hands under my shirt and we roll around on the ground.

The music from downstairs is booming through the door and it feels good to be away from all those scary older kids. Aiden doesn't make me feel nervous. He is still a boy.

Suddenly the room is flooded with light and Olivia's standing over us. 'Aiden, you can't fuck her, you're a child still—you wouldn't be able to get it up.' She grabs my arm and pulls me up from the floor, laughing and berating him. 'She's *my* friend. Get lost.'

I mumble a bit and the room is spinning around and around. Then everything goes black.

•

The morning sun is shining on my face and Olivia is shaking me.

'Mum's here. I called her to come get us. She says you stink of alcohol so she knows you got drunk. Let's just hope the smell of vodka has disappeared by the time we drop you home. Mum did say we can get Macca's for breakfast. That'll sort you out. Egg McMuffin . . . Yum. And hash browns.' She licks her lips. Her eyes are red and I wonder if she is still stoned.

She is right, though. The Macca's makes me feel better. Olivia looks at me in the back of the car and sniggers. 'I hope your mum doesn't smell the booze on ya.'

At home, I slip through the front door, hoping to make it to the bathroom unobserved, but Mum is vacuuming nearby.

'Hi, darling,' she shouts over the hum.

'Hey, Mum,' I mutter, trying to keep my distance.

I run up the stairs to my room and slam the door behind me, hoping she won't follow. I sit on my bed and look out the window. I think of Aiden and the older boys in that big house with no adults. Bra Boys is what everyone was calling them last night. I hate myself for how disgusting I feel. *I'm never drinking again*, I say to myself. I think of how much Dad drinks and wonder how he copes with feeling so dreadful all the time.

Maybe next time I'll smoke pot instead, I decide.

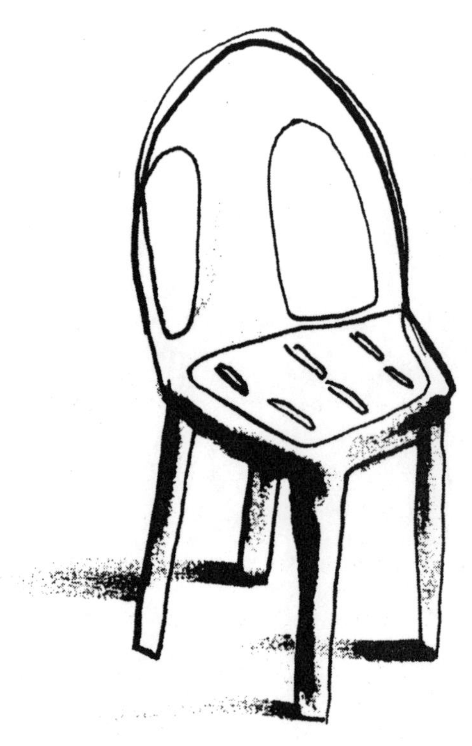

Statement

I sit on a rickety plastic chair beside my mum at the police station and fidget quietly. I have been preparing for this moment with my counsellor for the past few years—Mum sent me to see one after I told her about Garth. I went to a lot of kinesiology appointments as well. Mum's bangles clink together lightly as she reaches over to hold my hand and we sit in stillness together for what feels like a long time, waiting.

Finally the door opens and a male police officer dressed in a blue uniform comes in with a notepad and sits down at the table across from us. I look at the gun strapped to his hip. It looks heavy and big.

He looks at me. 'Hello, Bertie. My name is Detective James and I will be taking your statement this morning. I can see here in my notes that this is the second time you'll be making a statement, and that you made the first one a few years ago.' He flicks through the pages with his thumb, scanning some words I can't see.

He turns on a recording device, clicks his pen and addresses me again.

'I know this will be difficult, but I need you to tell me in as much detail as you can what happened. As much as you can remember, no matter how insignificant it might seem. Everything here is important.'

My tummy swirls, but I nod and, clinging to Mum's hand, start to speak.

As I talk, I start to remember small things I hadn't before. I describe the colour of the tiles in the bathroom, and the temperature of the bathwater. The flavour of ice cream. Then other things that I could never forget: the mustard-coloured curtains; the print on his pyjamas. The touching. What he said to me before and after. How he made me keep this secret. How he made me feel dirty. The smell in the room. The time of day.

I start to feel really sick. I can hear the sound of his breath loud in my ears as the words come tumbling out. My body feels hot and my skin stings and my eyes burn; I am reliving each moment as I describe it. But now, for the first time, I don't feel scared. The words don't frighten or confuse me. They make me feel angry. Violated. Stripped down. Hollow. Heavy like lead. Each word that comes out of my mouth feels like a loud footstep. I want to be able to be direct and strong and clear so my statement is the best it can be. I know what he did was wrong. It was a crime. It was not my fault. And he should go to jail.

Mum's hand grips mine.

I know that the other girls Garth abused have made police statements and that the police are preparing a case in order to charge him. I look down at the chair and wonder how they felt when they sat here like I am now. I imagine their mother, the neighbour with the blonde hair, holding their hands like my mother is holding mine.

I feel proud that I haven't cried.

Everyone says that paedophiles get murdered in jail. That they are the most hated of all the criminals.

I stare at the floor and I think of him saying, *Dirty girl. You like it.*

•

On the way home, Mum asks me if I want a treat. This word, this reward she wants to give me for being strong, doesn't make me feel good. Ice cream will never be the same.

'I'd love some apricot slice from Macro,' I say quietly. 'Or a rice ball.'

The leaves of the plane trees cast green and golden light on the pavement as we drive home.

Breath

Lately I have been feeling out of breath and my lungs feel like fists clenched tight. I inhale, and it's like there's not enough air to breathe. My lungs don't inflate. I breathe as deep as I can and imagine that I'm floating all the way to the top of my lungs . . . but my face squishes near my throat and I feel like I'm drowning. I remember the science teacher Mr Morton visiting our class last week with a lamb's lungs and blowing air into them to demonstrate how they work. They looked slippery and white. The class all went *ew* when he held them high above his head. I try to envisage

Mr Morton blowing air into the top of my lungs—but they are clogged full of thick fog and the oxygen can't get through.

Every day it seems to get worse. I stare off into the distance in maths class and inhale as deeply as I can but it just feels like there's nothing there. It's a dry desert with no wind.

I sit alone in bathroom cubicles at recess and lunch and hunt desperately for my breath, but it has evaporated. I gasp like a fish out of water. It's gone.

Afternoon light dapples the water as I lie in the bath and listen to the music blaring from the kitchen as Mum cooks dinner downstairs. Sting is singing about fields of barley and fields of gold. His voice reverberates through the floorboards and makes the bathwater vibrate. I love this song. I dip my ears underwater to see if it makes the music clearer but instead it sounds all muddled and muddy with the clanking of pots and cutlery underlining each word.

I come up for air but suddenly there's that tight feeling in my chest again. I inhale deeply but I can't seem to draw a breath. I'm not getting enough air. I start to panic . . . My pulse starts to quicken and now I am scared. Really scared. My heart is pounding against my ribs. My mouth is dry. I look around wildly. There is air everywhere, but I just can't seem to get it in. Why? Why is this easy for everyone else and not for me?

I start to cry.

Next thing I know Mum is in the bathroom.

'Mum, I can't breathe. I don't know what's wrong with me.'

I am panting between strangled breaths, trying to gulp the air.

'I can't breathe. I can't breathe. I can't breathe.'

Mum helps me out of the bath and wraps me in a towel. I feel dizzy.

'I'm taking you to hospital,' Mum says. 'It could be an asthma attack.'

And then we are in the car, speeding past the cafes and restaurants on Darlinghurst Road. Water drips into my eyes from my wet hair. I can taste the salt from my tears.

St Vincent's emergency room is packed but we are called in first. Apparently not being able to breathe trumps everything else.

A nurse puts an oxygen mask on me and the pounding of my heart starts to slow. I feel the thick air in my lungs suddenly turn cool and fresh and expansive—like an endless wide-open field. I can breathe again. Relief.

I can hear the doctor talking to Mum, telling her that it's not asthma and asking if I've ever had a panic attack before.

My mum shakes her head 'No. Nothing like this before.' She glances at me. She looks worried.

The doctor turns to me and asks if there is anything going on that has been making me stressed or anxious.

I shake my head . . . but inside my chest gets tight as I think about what Mum told me last week.

Garth is dead. He committed suicide. He gassed himself in his car in the garage.

I have been trying to weigh up my feelings about this ever since she told me. I don't feel sad. I don't feel anything except a little queasy. I wonder if his dog Hamish was gassed too. I wonder what it would have looked like. Him sitting alone on the brown leather upholstery in the front seat of his car. The dog next to him. In the dark. Holding on to the steering wheel.

Waiting for it to end. Did he feel guilty? Or was he afraid? *Coward*, I think. *He must have known the police were coming for him.* I wonder how the other children felt about it. Whether they care. I wonder how my aunty feels. They were close for a long time. Is she sad? Will there be a funeral? So many questions but I'm too numb to ask them.

'No,' I say. 'There's nothing I'm particularly stressed about.' I look the doctor in the eye for a moment and then look away.

The doctor gives me a paper bag. 'I want you to carry this in your pocket for a while. If you feel like you're getting out of breath again, tighten the open end like this'—he shows me what he means—'and then hold it up to your mouth and breathe in and out into the bag as best you can. Doing this means that you're recycling your oxygen and not taking so much in that you might faint. How do you feel about that?'

'Okay,' I say. 'Does this mean I don't get a puffer?' I have always secretly wanted one of those blue puffers that some of the kids used for sport. I tried it a few times and I like the way it makes me feel a little dizzy and how the air inside it was a bit cold.

'No,' says the doctor. 'Just the paper bag.'

As we leave the hospital I feel for the crease of the paper bag in my pocket and feel a little safer knowing it is there.

Rehab

I've been banned from going to Dad's house by myself. Mum says it's because of a lot of things. 'It's not a healthy environment for anyone to be around,' she says. Since then, Mum and Dad have been fighting a lot on the phone and I often see Mum crying. I don't see what the big problem is with me going there; I've seen worse. I just miss being able to have time alone with Dad.

Lately, Dad has been driving me up to the pub in Bondi Junction in the yellow Toyota Corolla to have 'special drinks' before lunchtime. I have the usual pink lemonade and Dad has a few beers and makes small talk with the barman and the other regulars. He always tells them that I'm too smart to go to school and that I'm going to be a painter like him and I can rap in Spanish. He swerves all over the road when he drives me home and I feel dizzy from all my sugary drinks. I've been instructed to tell someone when he is drunk, but he tells me a couple of beers is okay, and that it's our secret. 'It's okay to tell a white lie from time to time,' he says. I feel this is fair enough.

He was even back in rehab in Botany recently. I don't like it there. The drive is long and hot and you have to go past the airport down endless roads and past houses that all look the same. I don't understand how anyone could live somewhere so dull. There is also a beach nearby, but the water is swampy and the palm trees are half dead.

The rehab centre looks like a hospital or an old people's home. Last time we went Dad had just had his stomach pumped, and since then I haven't been able to get the image out of my mind. I keep imagining a crowd of people in flapping lab coats fussing around and holding toilet plungers to Dad's mouth . . . and of his stomach being cut open and them using a bike pump to get the alcohol out. It's messy and Dad is lying in an empty bath. I don't know what really happens when you get your stomach pumped but I'm too scared to ask anyone in case it is even worse than I imagine.

I wish he would just stop drinking.

•

Dad is only out of rehab for a few days before he starts drinking again. Victoria has announced to the family that she will be taking him to the Betty Ford Center in Los Angeles for two months. Apparently it's where all the broken-down American celebrities go to recover, but I just can't picture Dad there. That kind of fake grandeur doesn't fit with his lovely impishness.

While they are away, my school holds auditions for a big play called *The Journey*. We are moving campuses and the play will be about what our school has gone through to survive. I've started learning the drums, and even though I'm not the best drummer (yet), I play percussion in the high school jazz band. I'm the youngest member of the band, and I feel cool because I get to hang out with the older musicians who smoke cigarettes at lunchtime in the bushes at the park. Sometimes I join them, but I still just bum-puff and I think they might know it.

The final number of *The Journey* is a rendition of 'The Long and Winding Road' by The Beatles. I try out for the role of lead singer and I get it. Lately when I have been practising the drums at home I have been singing along and have been harbouring a secret desire to be a singer. When I told Mum I got the lead she was very surprised.

On the day of the full dress rehearsal the whole school is there to watch, as well as staff and parents. The school hall is packed. I wait backstage with the band. I've never sung with a microphone before and my hands are sweaty and shaking.

After an hour of anxious waiting, rushing to the toilet to wee every fifteen minutes, we're up.

Everyone is looking at me as I walk onto the stage.

I look for my mum and find her standing near the back of the room.

My heart is thumping and I almost vomit from the adrenaline.

But as soon as I open my mouth and sing the first few words, all my fear falls away. I feel my chest vibrate with each note and the room feels liquid. All my anxiety and pain and fear and hurt are squeezed into each note and it just feels so good. I can turn my feelings into sound. It's magic.

To sing of the feeling of being alone on a winding road full of memories and dreams . . . that there is hope for me, even, waiting behind an imaginary door.

I can hear the drums crash and the last hit of cymbal, and the flutes and clarinets trill their final notes. The audience erupts in applause.

My eyes water in relief.

This is where I want to be forever.

This is me.

Everything is different

I'm sitting in maths class, staring at my teacher's toupee as he tries to explain algebra to us. A equals B except after C, which equals X Y Z . . . *which equals b-o-r-i-n-g*, I say to myself, and I doodle another frog cartoon on the front of my exercise book.

The teacher's droning is interrupted by a tap at the door. A staff member from the front office enters the classroom and walks over to my teacher, whispering something hurriedly in his ear.

The teacher looks at me. 'Bertie, can you please pack up your things and go and wait at reception for your mum? She is picking you up early today.'

'Okay, sure,' I say. I quickly gather my books as the rest of the class watches, envious that I get to leave early.

I walk downstairs and notice the new laminate floor already has scuff marks on it. We've only just moved to the new campus and the building works aren't quite finished. The playground is a concrete slab with barbed wire around it and basketball rings at either end.

As I drop my bag at my feet in the office, the receptionist gives me a sympathetic look and says my mum won't be long.

I stare at my Doc Martens and trace the yellow lacing around the front of the boot and note where I've coloured some stitching in black to make it look uneven. I tap the toes together nervously.

I can't shake this feeling in the pit of my stomach that something is wrong.

Mum never picks me up from school. I always get the bus home. *Always.*

I think about Dad and everything that has been going on lately. He's been in and out of rehab so many times. It's been hard to be near him; he seems so sad and angry at the same time. Recently he fell down the stairs and cut his face open. He had to get twenty stitches across his nose and cheek. Mum went over to help him and when I went over a few days later there was still a big bloodstain on the carpet from where he landed.

Hot tears fall down my own cheeks. I suddenly feel certain something has happened to Dad.

I just . . . know.

I can't find him in my thoughts.

I see our white Tarago pull up out the front. Mum leaps out of it and comes bounding towards the school office. I can tell she has been crying.

This is it.

Dad is dead.

This is the moment she will tell me he is gone.

I hold my breath.

Mum walks into the office and looks at me, her face pale.

'Bertie, your father has had a heart attack and he is in a coma. We don't know if he is going to wake up. Felix is in the car already. I'm taking you straight to the hospital.'

She is blurry through my tears. There is a loud ringing in my ears. But around us, the world has gone completely quiet.

No one speaks on the drive to the hospital. My brother sniffles and looks out the window.

•

The hospital corridors are full of people and I can see their mouths moving but the ringing in my ears is still so loud I can't hear anything else.

We walk into a waiting room and I see Victoria is there already, but her back is turned to me.

I hate her.

She left Dad recently and he's been all alone. I feel my face flush red.

Auguste comes in with his wife Andrea, and he speaks to Mum and points in the direction of the intensive care ward.

Mum takes my hand and squeezes it and holds my brother's hand too. We walk into a big room full of beeping machines. Dad is in a bed at the far end. I can see his little shape under the outline of the sheets. He seems so small and fragile. There is a tube going into his mouth and his eyes are open and looking straight up at the ceiling. Mum says I can hold his hand.

'You can talk to him if you like, darling,' she says. 'He can hear you.'

I take his hand and look at his eyes. They twitch from side to side. I look up to see what he can see, and then I lean over and whisper to him, 'I think there's some spaghetti on the ceiling, Dad.' But he doesn't respond.

•

That week I don't have to go to school. Mum says the doctors have told her that he won't wake up. So we go in to the hospital every day and sit with him after my siblings have been there. He is never alone and that makes me feel a bit better. I don't want him to be alone.

I start writing a song on a guitar that my brother brought home recently. I've been teaching myself how to play and it's helping me. Even just holding it makes the emotional chaos go away.

One morning we go in to see Dad, and Mum says she will leave me alone with him for a few minutes in case there's anything I'd like to say.

It's good to be on my own with Dad finally, but I'm a bit scared. I don't know what to say. It feels like if I speak I'll intrude on the beeping and the sound of the machine that's helping him to breathe. Like my words won't be able to penetrate all these mechanical barriers. I take a deep breath, and speak anyway.

'Dad, I'm here. It's Beatrice Octavia. I love you. Please don't leave. Please come back. I love you. I need you.'

I look at him and then press my face against the side of the bed.

Dad squeezes my hand.

My heart skips a beat.

He moved. They said he would never move or wake up again. 'Dad?'

Suddenly his arm flails and he is trying to rip out the tubes, gasping. Then he is reaching for me with both arms, trying to hug me. The machines start to beep urgently and the doctors run over.

'Dad, I'm here. It's okay.'

He grips my hand and looks at me, tears streaming down his cheeks.

•

The doctors said that he wouldn't wake up, but he did.

Then the doctors said he would never walk again. But when we drove him home from the hospital, Dad pushed the car door open and gestured to the wheelchair there ready for him. 'Get that thing out of my way.'

He stands up, pauses to get his balance, then strides proudly through his front door.

My irrepressible Dad, made of shadows and lines. Part cat, part bird, part magic—all mine.

Coda

On our mantelpiece is a book that was given to my son recently. It is called: *What is Love?* I find myself staring at it, asking myself the same question, as it is one that has resonated through my own book. What is love? Is this what love is?

It is such a simple word, only four letters, yet in my experience love is anything but simple, and it is certainly not straightforward.

In reliving my childhood memories, I have discovered a world of magic and wonder—but I have had to enter a place of darkness, too. And it is in the space between the light and the shadow, in the grey tones, that I began to explore the relationship I had with my father. Ours was a deep, complex love, one without limits or confines. I adored him, but he had serious problems with alcohol—and, as a result, with boundaries.

For all that was beautiful and tender, I have had to deal with feelings of confusion and sadness and betrayal. My innocence was lost too young, and too abruptly. As a result, I have had great difficulty trusting people with whom I have intimate relationships, and I very rarely feel safe. I often feel alone and isolated. But these feelings have also made me resilient. They have caused me to reach deep inside myself, and it's in the reaching that I have become strong. With every tough time I get through, I grow more powerful. Art has been essential to me through this process, as I find new ways to use my voice, to express myself. I write music, and I write prose. Like my father, I draw and paint.

Shortly after Dad recovered from his coma, he was diagnosed with alcohol-related dementia. As a result, I was never able to talk to him about what happened, and why it happened, and I spent much of the two decades that followed wishing I could. But in the final hours of his life I was able to sit with him in the quietness, and in the grey light I held his hand and looked into his eyes and we met there. I know he heard what I had to say, and that has brought me peace. From this peace, forgiveness has followed. I am able to observe everything that was and everything that is, and just be with it.

And in the deafening silence of what is left behind, I hear echoes: tumbling down musical stairs, clanking pots and pans, spinning in charcoal dust and splatters of paint. My childhood world was full of cracks. Full of light and full of dark. But it was full of love.

I look at my own child now, who was conceived exactly a year after my father passed. There's a sparkle of Dad in my little boy, and he fills my heart with a new love—perhaps the greatest love of all.

Acknowledgements

First, I would like to thank my mother: you never doubted me when I told you what I'd been through, not once. I could always depend on your support and your embrace when I needed them most—you are like a lifeboat on a turbulent sea. I was always aware of how hard it would be for you to read this book, to read in such detail about your child experiencing things no child ever should, and this awareness deepened even further when I became a mother myself. But while it may cause you pain, I hope that it will be healing for you as well, and that we will be able to talk about it more easily. Thank you for taking me to a range of different therapies through all my various ages and stages of life: the kinesiology, the counselling, the chi gong, the meditation, the psychologists and the psychiatrists. The yoga and the long walks on the beach. Thank you for helping me find the courage to be the person and the artist that I dreamed of being and have become. It is because of you that I found the strength to find these words and speak my truth.

To my son Rumi, who protected me in my tummy as I wrote. Your kicks and hiccups reminded me of the miracle that is life itself. You've shown me a new way of loving.

To my beautiful partner Mandy: you are everything to me. Thank you for just being there—and for being the person you are. I know it has been hugely challenging for you to watch me relive my pain. I really appreciate your patience and understanding.

To my GG Ramona. Thank you for letting me come downstairs to your apartment and write. For letting me weep on your shoulder and talk through the myriad thoughts in my head. For supplying all the rosehip tea a woman could want!

To my brother Felix, who has been quietly waiting to read the book—thank you for being such an extraordinary human and a deeply loving and loyal brother. I know you're always in my corner, and that means the world to me. You were there through a lot of these experiences, and I expect it will bring a lot up for you. But I will always be here to talk about it whenever you need me.

Thank you to Cookie, a new member of our family. Your support and your soft and true-hearted nature are very grounding and such a gift in my life.

To my agent, Grace Heifetz, who came to my flat every week to be my guide and my (sometimes) counsellor through the writing of this book. Your unwavering support, your great compassion and your much-needed doses of laughter were magnificent. So too were all the pastries you brought to fulfil my pregnancy cravings! We haven't drunk nearly enough wine yet, my friend. And thank you for connecting me with the wonderful Jane Palfreyman, publisher and woman extraordinaire. I look forward to the many dinners we will share and more books to come!

Thank you to Ali Lavau for your wonderful and thoughtful edit. I felt really held and safe in this space with you. Thank you to Samantha Kent, for seeing the book to fruition. You've been fantastic in what has been some tricky territory.

I would like to acknowledge the Gadigal people of the Eora Nation, the traditional custodians of the land on which this book was written and published, and pay my respects to the Elders both past and present. Sovereignty has never been ceded. Always was, always will be, Aboriginal land.